HOW TO
BEAT
THE S.A.T.

AND

ALL STANDARDIZED
MULTIPLE-CHOICE
TESTS

HOW TO BEAT THE S.A.T.

AND

ALL STANDARDIZED MULTIPLE-CHOICE TESTS

MICHAEL DONNER

WORKMAN PUBLISHING, NEW YORK

ACKNOWLEDGMENTS

With thanks to John Boswell for the idea, Suzanne Rafer for the direction, Wendy Palitz for the clarity, and Peter Workman for the vision.

M.D.

Library of Congress Cataloging in Publication Data

Donner, Michael.
  How to beat the SAT.

  1. Scholastic aptitude test—Study guides.
I. Title.
LB2353.57.D66   378′.1662   80-54618
ISBN 0-89480-154-6 (pbk.)   AACR2

Cover and Book Design: Wendy Palitz
Diagrams: Ludvik Tomazic

Manufactured in the United States of America
First printing June 1981
10 9 8 7 6 5 4 2

CONTENTS

PART 1

HOW TO TAKE A TEST

THE TESTING GAME

Taking standardized tests is, for most people, an anxiety-laden ordeal that must be undergone at one time or another.

About 1.5 million people take the Scholastic Aptitude Test (SAT) every year, and millions more take similar tests such as the Graduate Record Examination (GRE), Civil Service Exams, and IQ tests. If the stakes were not so serious—acceptance to college, to professional school, to the professions themselves—these tests would simply be annoying intrusions in one's life.

But as we all know, *they matter*, even to the point of determining our future course in life and in some cases, regrettably, our own self-esteem.

Yet, as serious as the tests might be, taking tests remains in essence a *game*. This is not a metaphor; it is a fact. In a game, a player wins not merely because he has more knowledge, or desire, or preparation, or luck, but because he knows his game inside out.

Good test takers, like good game players, don't even blink when they find themselves in uncharted territory. On the contrary, they revel in the knowledge that, though others may stumble, they will find a way, because they are armed with a method and with the confidence that method instills. This book is about that method.

THE TWO KINDS OF KNOWLEDGE

There are many ways to prepare for a game—or for a test. It stands to reason that some ways are more effective than others. If a small body of subject matter is all that's involved, the obvious best strategy is simply to know it *all*, cold. To force a win or a draw at tic-tac-toe, for example, you need only memorize a few basic sequences of moves. But the more varied and broad-based the body of material that will be tested, the less effective will be your efforts to master it.

In the case of most standardized achievement tests, eleventh-hour cramming can be of some use, but its value diminishes as the breadth and complexity of the subject area increase. For most aptitude tests, which are not *about* any subject area but draw their questions from all over the lot, last-minute study is naturally of less value still—and in many cases no value at all.

And yet—ironically, incredibly—you will find in any large bookstore a legion of official-looking "guides" to preparation for just these kinds of aptitude and achievement tests, many of them 500-to-600-page volumes crammed with knowledge and sample tests; and you will find in the Yellow Pages of most phone directories numerous test-preparation schools charging $300 and more for an intensive ten-week course.

I am not saying that these books and schools are entirely worthless; if you give the books a great deal of diligent effort, or the schools a great deal of time and money, they will probably have some small impact on your score. But it is worth noting that even the best of the schools make no guarantee as to your eventual performance. They only claim, in the vaguest possible terms, that their methods will produce "results" and will "make a difference."

How to Beat the SAT is unique in that is does not offer formidable encyclopedic knowledge on the infinite variety of testable material; indeed it hardly even deals with the *material* at all. Instead, it concentrates on a simple game plan. This plan consists of a few basic principles and is designed to offer a maximum return for a minimum of preparation effort. Rather than waste your time, energy, and money, I have condensed all the information that will definitely enhance your score into an intentionally small manual, and have thrown out all the tedious permutations of cramming—cramming which might net you a handful of extra correct answers but also might drive you to distraction, and profit you nothing.

KNOW YOUR OPPONENT

It may come as a surprise to you that your opponent in the testing game is not your fellow test taker—the genius in the next seat who could ace you out of acceptance at Yale—but the *test maker* himself. As a prospective test taker, you must study the test maker's tricks and resources until you know them inside out. One way to do this is to take a lot of tests. It is a well-known fact that performances improve with experience.

But if you take this route, you are liable to learn too little too late, and in most cases your bad scores will be weighed equally with your good ones. Clearly you need a shortcut. (The commercially produced dry-run tests provided in the guidebooks and by the schools are inadequate because they are thin imitations; they are not made by the *real* test maker and they are often concocted simply to impress the student with the value of the course materials. They can—inadvertently but inexcusably—produce a false sense of confidence and lead to a shatteringly rude awakening on the real D-Day.) Faster, easier, and more effective is to make a concerted study of the test maker himself—his strategic ploys and the landscape of his game board. These are the sole concerns of this book. You will simply be zeroing in on the things that many people would eventually intuit for themselves if left to their own devices, and take them one step further by absorbing them as *rules.**

The best way to familiarize yourself with a Rule is to follow carefully the explanations of the sample problems and attempt to solve the practice questions by applying the Rule as it is given, and by no other means. Thus it will be helpful, temporarily, to suspend your direct knowledge of how to solve the problem in favor of applying only the indirect technique described in the Rule formation. (But, of course, in a real test you must first exhaust the direct approach before resorting to the use of Rules.)

There will be nothing difficult to memorize—just a few common-sense rules about how to recognize a winning move and take maximum advantage of probability and logic. With these rules we will squeeze out that competitive edge which—in its cumulative effect—will lift your score far beyond what the test maker intended.

I realize that this is a big claim; the standardized tests

---

*Not all kinds of test questions are equally vulnerable to strategic attack. Some are more vulnerable than others and some, it should be said, are virtually invulnerable. Although this book can't unlock *all* doors, by mastering it you stand to gain as much as a 10, 20, or 30 percentile test edge.

have long been considered "unbreakable." But the approach you will be taking is a revolutionary one. A simple experiment will prove that the methods presented in this book can definitely improve one's performance, and by a really substantial amount: Anyone who is able and willing to take (or has already taken) a sample test before reading this book and then a different version of the same test after reading this book will not fail to be impressed. (If you plan to do this, do the first part now, to be fair, before reading farther.) Indeed to my great satisfaction, when I took a series of six SAT-Math tests (enough to be statistically definitive), while applying only *five* of the principles in this book (Rules 2, 3, 5, 6, and 7) and *without even looking at the questions* but only at the answer choices, my average score per test was 140 points higher than random guessing would have produced, and higher than one-quarter of what all test takers (test takers who benefited by looking at the questions) actually do score.

SAT AS A MODEL

The main text of this book is based on the Scholastic Aptitude Test (SAT) prepared by the Educational Testing Service (ETS) of Princeton, N.J., in conjunction with the College Entrance Examination Board. Special sections follow, which extend and modify the SAT rules for use on the following: Preliminary Scholastic Aptitude Test (PSAT), National Merit Scholarship Qualifying Test (NMSQT), College Board Achievement Tests, Advanced Placement Program and College Level Examination Program (AP/CLEP), Graduate Record Examinations (GRE), the American College Testing Program (ACT), the Miller Analogies Test (MAT), Medical College Admissions Test (MCAT), Dental Admissions Test (DAT), nursing exams sponsored by the National League for Nursing and the Psychological Corporation, Law School Admission Test (LSAT), Graduate Management Admission Test (GMAT), the National Teacher Exam (NTE), the Professional and Administrative Career Exam (PACE), Secondary School Aptitude Test (SSAT), the Test of General Educational Development (GED), New York State Regents Examinations, and the Test of English as a Foreign Language (TOEFL).

I have focused primarily on the SAT because it is the most widely taken test, and its structure is fairly typical of all the others. Differences in structure (and corresponding differences in rules) for each of the other tests are fully explained in the various sections at the end. If you are *not* taking the SAT, it is necessary to study and master only those sections devoted to the test you are planning to take. However, you are encouraged to read the entire book because it will help you to round out your intuitive arsenal and develop what the ETS calls "testwiseness." The more types of questions and Rules you are exposed to, the more resourceful you will be at zeroing in on your test's weaknesses.

HOW TO USE THIS BOOK

Each of the principles or techniques that comprise my "system" is formulated as a Rule. Each Rule is presented with illustrative examples and, once explained, with additional sample problems to test your understanding of it. I will explain why each Rule works, how to apply it, when to rely on it, and when to be wary of its limitations. Where possible, I will employ questions from actual tests. When I am forced to modify them I will do so without compromising their essential authenticity. Some Rules are accompanied by Memory Aids. When the written out Rule seems too long to keep in mind I have devised a catchy, abbreviated form to help you keep it in mind.

The structure of this book was carefully planned to give you the greatest possible ease in acquiring basic skills.

1. Carefully read the chapter on Strategy and Tactics and the pertinent Rules for the particular test you are taking.

2. After reading once through the Rules, review any which you feel you haven't quite grasped. It is not necessary to be able to recall the number of any Rule, but simply to master its basic concept and have an idea of its relative importance.

3. Having reread any Rules that you were unable to recall in step 2, look them *all* over again, making sure each is familiar. This level of familiarity will be quite sufficient for most people in the heat of battle. (The structures of the test questions themselves will jog your memory and be your ally!) Any further attempt to distill, memorize, or otherwise manipulate the material will probably not have any effect; *understanding* alone is the key.

4. On the morning or evening before your test session, repeat step 2 and, if necessary, step 3.

PREPARATION AND ATTITUDE

As for any other preparation techniques you may wish to employ, I purposely do not offer any suggestions. Indeed, my only advice is "don't be a victim of advice." Much that passes for advice in this area is worthless or even destructive, so don't work yourself up into making preparations that differ from your normal habits. For example, there is no reason to believe that going to bed abnormally early the night before a test will improve your performance. It could just as easily make you a bit dull. Eating a "good" breakfast, if you're not used to having one, could slow you down too. Attempting to alter your physical or mental condition with *unusual* diet, exercise, or artificial stimulants could lead to a transcendental experience, but there's no knowing what it may do to your bottom line. So relax.

Of course it will be wise to read the test maker's preparatory bulletin, *Taking the SAT*, and study the sample questions just to minimize the effect of surprise and unfamiliarity during the test itself; and the experiment suggested earlier (taking sample tests before and after reading this book), though not essential, can be useful both to confirm your confidence in the techniques you will have acquired here and to familiarize yourself with the "feel" of the test. In reading the sample questions that I provide with each Rule, you may get the false impression that the real test is going to be easy. Although considerable care has been taken to select questions that are representative of a real test, it is impossible to simulate accurately the conditions of a real test session. Make no mistake: The time pressure, the unrelenting barrage of hundreds of questions, the hardbacked chair, the ritual of the booklets and answer sheets, and the atmosphere of everyone else's nervous energy will be a very different kind of experience and will take its toll. Some tension is natural and desirable, and it will help you to remain alert, cautious, and diligent.

The most important thing to understand in using this system is that, as a test taker, you really are playing a game—or solving a puzzle, if you prefer. Realizing this should help to relax and encourage you and remind you that you have a broader range of resources to call upon than your "opponent" may have counted on.

■■■■

STRATEGY AND TACTICS

This section is a distillation of everything that matters in terms of your general approach to the test. In places it may seem reminiscent of "advice" found elsewhere, but it contains vital guidelines for making the most effective use of the Rules in the sections that follow.

BE CLEAR

Adopt a clear, logical approach to problem-solving. Every question is a problem, a puzzle with one and only one correct solution. If at all possible, make sure you have a lock on the right answer first. There is, of course, no substitute for certainty. The Rules in the following sections are strictly for use when certainty eludes you and guessing is necessary. Then guess if you must, and guess methodically.

Because the tests are made for a mass "audience," the intended correct answer will rarely be overly abstruse or profound. Rather, the key will almost invariably be making the "right" mental connection. If you come up with a really original, clever, and clearly offbeat solution, don't trust it. Look instead for Everyman's answer.

For example: After eliminating three obviously wrong answers, your choices for the antonym of *amiable* boil down to either *nervous* or *churlish*.

The answer is, strictly, neither of these, but the task is to pick the best of a bad lot. You reason that nervous, uptight people are not amiable (after all, they rarely command *your* affection), and you're right—but that's too clever. The fact that churlish, vulgar people are not infrequently good-natured must be overlooked if you're to get the intended right answer: Churlish!

On the other hand, intentionally misleading questions (a la "Which weighs more, a pound of feathers or a pound of lead?") are quite common in standardized tests.

The lesson to be learned from these two examples is never to take anything for granted.

BE ECONOMICAL

Use your time and energy wisely. On most tests, all correct answers are equal in point value, no matter how difficult or time consuming to arrive at. This point is often lost on the test taker during the heat of battle.

Know which types of questions can be answered most quickly. For example, the ETS tells you right out that on the SAT-Verbal test, "Antonyms usually take the least time, followed by analogies, sentence completion answers, and, finally, the reading comprehen-

THE DIRECT ROUTE

Since the test maker usually assumes that you will be working at breakneck speed, be very wary of his fooling you into embarking on any long or complex calculation. On most general tests, there is almost always a simple route to the correct answer. If none appears, skip the question and plan to return to it later.

sion questions." But a little experience with the last mentioned will tell you that they are *significantly* more time consuming, are best solved in clusters, and should be saved until you've made at least one complete pass over the rest of the section you are working on. When appropriate, divide your time allocation by the number of questions in order to get a rough idea of how to pace yourself. Thus, if you have thirty minutes to answer thirty questions, you would need to answer, on average, one question a minute. In general, work as rapidly as possible *without* sacrificing thoroughness and care.

One sure answer is almost always worth more than two guesses.

BE METICULOUS

Exercise extreme care at all times, both in the reasoning process and in recording answers. Read preliminary directions carefully, familiarizing yourself with them ahead of time if possible. It is a sad fact that more mistakes are made out of carelessness than out of ignorance. It could fairly be said that standardized tests have a built-in "cultural" bias against people who tend to be sloppy and inattentive.

BE SYSTEMATIC

There are numerous approaches to use for squeezing the maximum number of correct answers out of a test, but the one that works best with this system is the following five-stage attack:

1. One brisk but unhurried reading of the entire test (or section), entering only those answers that come without straining, and skipping over all others without regret. (In many tests, each subsection is arranged so that it builds to a generally increasing level of difficulty. When you hit strong resistance on two or three questions in a row, you may want to skip to the beginning of the next subsection and plan to return later.) The idea here is to fatten up your "CATS" ratio—that is, to keep your Correct-Answers-to-Time-Spent ratio as high as possible at all times. Your CATS should run as far ahead of your time allocation as possible. It is unwise to linger over any problem so long as there are still questions available that may be answered more quickly.

2. A second reading, allowing a few moments more per question, but only if the knot seems to be unraveling. Your CATS will slow down a bit here, but that is as it should be.

3. A third reading, selecting the questions that seem most attainable—either by direct solving or by the indirect methods we will be taking up in the sections following—and concentrating on them. If you still have a fat CATS ratio, you can be quite deliberate here. If time pressure does not seem to be a major factor after the third reading, check all answers carefully, consider them carved in granite, and plan not to return again to any question already completed. If time pressure is a factor, ignore this procedure.

4. The fourth reading is in a way the most crucial, because it is here that you will proceed to leave the test maker in the dust. You have already answered the questions he was expecting you to answer based on your level of intelligence and/or preparation. Now is the time for "over-

achieving" by cracking the tough nuts, returning to the doubtful cases, and applying all methods at your disposal, especially for guessing. Much of your real struggle will probably take place during the fourth reading, and often involves a significant number of questions. Don't let this dismay you; it is as it should be. Seriously and actively attempt all questions for which time permits.

5. (Bail-out time!) Plan to use the last 10 or 15 percent of your time allocation (in most cases, five minutes or so) exclusively to venture guesses and fill in as many remaining blank spaces as possible. This procedure should preempt your efforts on whichever stage you happen to be working on, but you will most probably be well into stage 4 by this time anyway. Bail-out is a most critical period, when you can put to maximum effect many of the Rules following. It is not a time for panic, but for orderly, strategic withdrawal.

If you have answered all questions and have time left, you should still think of yourself as being in the bail-out phase. You can use your time to continue checking and rechecking answers if you have the least bit of doubt. Remain actively engaged until the buzzer rings, but stick with first impressions unless you have a compelling

reason to change them. It is inadvisable to leave a test— even a "completed" test—before the time is up, and it is especially foolish when despair or bravado is the motivation.

Note: There is nothing sacrosanct about the five-stage method. Many people will feel more comfortable combining stages 1, 2, and 3 in various ways and will be able to do so without seriously hurting their CATS. The difference among these stages is often slight anyway. But the proper use of stages 4 and 5 is essential if you wish to get the maximum benefit out of the system.

BE SAVVY

As already mentioned, intelligent guessing is the key to this system. It is essential that you know the odds; this is what really separates the sheep from the goats. If there's no penalty for guessing, you certainly can't afford *not* to guess. If there is a penalty, you still can't afford not to guess, but you must guess within certain well-defined limits. Strictly speaking, there is never a penalty for guessing; the penalty is only for guessing incorrectly, and it is equal to the penalty for giving a wrong answer you were sure was right. This is an important point and not simply a matter of semantics. In the SAT, PSAT, and GRE, for example, you score one "raw" point for each correct answer regardless of how you arrived at it, nothing for no answer, and minus ¼ point (on five-choice questions) for each wrong answer. Thus the difference between a right guess and a wrong guess is not 1 point but 1¼ points.

However, being able to definitely eliminate even one of five multiple-choice answers to a given question narrows the average range between a sure right answer and a guess from 1.00 to 0.94 and increases your guessing odds by 25 percent; eliminating two answer choices from contention increases your odds by 67 percent and eliminating three increases them by 150 percent. (Positively eliminating four answer choices is tantamount to positively identifying the single correct answer and is no longer an occasion for guessing.) Table I (page 20) shows the complete structure of odds that prevail under the various categories of guessing in an SAT-type situation and projects bonus score results in each category.

It should be noted that these bonuses outlined in Table I are the ones a mindless robot would enjoy. By using the various additional techniques for guessing presented in the sections that follow, and by using your native intelligence, the numbers in this table will increase substantially.

Another inference that can be made from Table I is that guessing is not an occasion for squeamishness. Guessing is, of course, not as good as certainty, but over the long haul you can count on your guesses accumulating like money in the bank to the approximate extent indicated in the table.

TACTICS: THE INDIRECT METHOD

Tactics, as I conceive them in relation to taking tests, are any and all manipulations of the test material other than a direct frontal attack based on your knowledge of the question. (A frontal attack is a tactic too, but you already know what you know, and you will be able to answer many questions correctly without any help from this book.) Taken all together and working as a system, these tactics constitute a potent "indirect" method, which—although it can never take the place of the direct application of your knowledge—can nevertheless be extremely useful for corroborating your knowledge, for confirming your suspicions, and, as a last resort, for saving the day when direct methods are getting you nowhere at all on a particular question.

THE GUESSING ODDS ON FIVE-PART MULTIPLE CHOICE QUESTIONS

	Complete Uncertainty	Relative Uncertainty (the intelligent guessing range)			Complete Certainty
A No. of choices eliminated	0	1	2	3	4
B No. of choices left	5	4	3	2	1
C Probable no. of correct ans. per 100 questions guessed at random	20	25	33	50	100
D Improvement in guessing odds	0%	25%	67%	150%	Absolute
E Resulting bonus earned per 100 questions	0	6	17	37	100 pts.
F Resulting gain in final score on typical SAT	0	30	100	230	600 pts.

When you have a lock on the correct answer, ignore indirect methods entirely. But when you haven't a clue, make full use of all tactics that apply. Between the two extremes, keep tactics in the near background and bring them to bear with cautious common sense. In presenting each tactical principle on

HOW TO READ THIS TABLE

Given any number of answer choices that you are positively able to eliminate (row A), there will remain in a five-part multiple-choice question the number of answer choices shown directly under in row B.

The vertical rows show the resulting data for the extremes of complete uncertainty and complete certainty and, given a random sample of one hundred questions and the effects of random probability, establish the limits of twenty and one hundred correct answers respectively.

If on these hypothetical one hundred questions you found yourself consistently in any one of three "intelligent guessing range" categories and guessed randomly from among the answers that remained, you would on average score the number of correct hits shown on the corresponding line in row C. The increase in your guessing odds for each category of *relative* uncertainty (1, 2, and 3 answer choices eliminated), when compared to your guessing odds under complete uncertainty, is shown on the corresponding line in row D. The resulting average bonus score earned by guessing—assuming neither good nor bad luck—is shown in row E.

This increase in raw score, when prorated to a full, typical SAT exam would result in the approximate net gain in overall score shown in row F.

Of course, in real life you would never find yourself consistently in any one category, but your experience will necessarily be a blend of all five categories, and will in most cases average somewhere between the third and fourth vertical rows.

the pages that follow, I will outline (via examples and practice questions) what "common sense" consists of in relation to it. When I advise you to "favor" a particular kind of answer, I mean that all other things being equal and there being no other clues to help you, choose that answer. There is, of course, no absolute guarantee that that answer will turn out to be correct, but history and the odds mildly—and in some cases strongly—favor it.

Conversely, when I say "avoid" a particular kind of answer, I mean that unless you have some other reason not to eliminate it from consideration, don't choose it; choose any of the others that remain in contention. Again, nothing is guaranteed, but you'll be making a good gamble by following this advice. And, short of knowing the answers, the more good gambles you take, the higher your overall score will be. That's the name of the game.

Each Rule that follows can in itself increase your score significantly. The 140-point average gain I referred to in The Testing Game made use of only a few of them. (The guessing bonuses outlined in Table I, page 20, depend on no rules at all—only the realities of statistical probability.) When coordinated with one another and, of course, with a careful study of the question, the Rules become all the more powerful.

You will notice that the Rules progress from the more general to the more specific. The reason for this is: The lower a Rule's number, the less relative weight it has. All the rules are valid, but some are more statistically potent than others. In the absence of *any* indications of right or wrong answers (a rare case) use Rule 1. If, as is likely, there is a conflict between two or more Rules, favor the Rule with the highest number.

The sixteen Rules that follow apply primarily to the SAT but no less—in various combinations—to a great number of other standardized tests. If you are an SAT candidate, proceed directly to Rule 1, on page 26. If you are a candidate for a test other than the SAT, before proceeding further read the section of this book that applies to the test you are taking (see the table of contents), and then refer only to those Rules which are there recommended for your particular test.

Rules 1 through 7 make use almost exclusively of the *answer choices only* and virtually ignore the material in the question itself. Rules 8 through 11, on the other hand, *do* make use of information given in the question, albeit in a highly unconventional way. Moreover, Rules 9 through 11 are not guessing techniques at all, but completely reliable auxiliary means for *determining* the correct answer. They have the additional virtue of enabling you to test empirically many of the answers you may have arrived at by any of the roundabout means in Rules 1–7.

■■■■■■

PART 2

THE SCHOLASTIC APTITUDE TEST

The SAT consists of three sections: the Math SAT, the Verbal SAT, and the Test of Standard Written English (TSWE).

The Math SAT consists of two question types: standard multiple-choice questions and quantitative comparisons.

The Verbal SAT consists of four question types: antonyms, analogies, sentence completions, and reading comprehension questions.

The TSWE consists of two question types: questions on sentence corrections and usage. Strictly speaking it is not really a part of the SAT. (Its purpose is to indicate what level of English composition course you should be placed in as a college freshman.) Your TSWE score is not *supposed* to be used by college administrators to determine your acceptibility for admission, but they can't help but see it when they look at your SAT scores, since all are reported on the same sheet of paper. Best to take it as seriously as the SAT itself.

RULE

1

GENERAL
RULE

TAME A WILD GUESS

- Avoid the ACE columns, especially C.
- Avoid identical answers on successive questions.

MEMORY AID:

Avoid Aces, Pairs, and Triplets

WHY THIS RULE WORKS

As you may be aware, on any given question the laws of random probability (*i.e.*, chance) make no answer column any more likely to contain the correct answer than any other answer column. However, many test makers have shown a strong tendency to meddle with the laws of pure chance. There is a good reason for this tendency. They have a vested interest in making sure that no desperate guesser is able, through sheer good luck, to score appreciably higher on the test than he would have by dint of his ability or his knowledge alone. They could not afford to have their test viewed by the public as a potential crap shoot.

The test makers presumably have figured out that wild guessers, like roulette players, put their money—and keep putting their money—on one or more favorite columns. Evidently because there is something comforting about the idea of symmetry, the columns most frequently selected by wild guessers are the middle column and, to a lesser extent, the two columns at the ends. That is, in five-answer questions, wild guessers choose columns *c*, *a*, and *e* the most frequently.

If you would like to verify this phenomenon, ask a few dozen people to pick a letter from *a* to *e*, and you'll be impressed by how many more than three-fifths of them pick *a*, *c*, or *e*. And if you ask them to pick a *series* of letters, you will find that they repeat their answers with more than random frequency.

I don't know whether the real test makers have conducted similar experiments, but they certainly behave as if they have. Or perhaps they are simply good intuitive psychologists. But whatever the reason, the test maker *does* put appreciably fewer correct answers in columns *a*, *c*, and *e* than the laws of chance would have them contain. Moreover, he puts two or more successive correct answers in any one given column much less frequently than statistical probability. Perhaps he thinks he is being clever by adopting this "strategy" against you, and in fact he *is* being clever—at least until you've learned his trick. But for you who know his trick, his cleverness makes him that much more vulnerable to the very tactic he set out to prevent you from using: wild guessing. So when guessing wildly, go against your natural tendency to choose *ace* and to choose duplicate answers in neighboring questions.

When I put this Rule to the acid test on a number of real standardized examinations of various types, I found that a comparison of the test maker's correct answer letters on the actual answer keys against the behavior of purely random distribution supported it with near-uniform consistency. In the case of the test reproduced in full in the widely available brochure, *Taking the SAT*, distributed by the College Entrance Examination Board, the results were fairly typical. They are tabulated in full in Table II (facing page).

HOW AND WHEN TO USE THIS RULE

It will not be difficult to remember to avoid answering columns *a*, *c*, and *e* (the columns at the ends and in the middle). As it turns out, several of the Rules that follow, such as Rules 2, 3, and 4, though unrelated, will by their own inner logic generally help to reinforce this idea. Applying the idea of avoiding pairs and triplets will depend largely on how certain you are of the answers to preceding or following questions. If you have a lock on either or both of those answers, you are actually in possession of useful information. Simply avoid repeating that letter or those letters, especially if either or both of them is an *a*, *c*, or *e*.

Use this Rule only when you have no better information,

HOW TO READ THIS TABLE

The SAT test referred to actually contained 195 questions of which 20 were not of the five-answer choice format and are therefore inapplicable here. In calculating how many times "pairs" and "triplets" occur, no carryover was made from one to another of the test's five discrete sections (though if this had been done, the effect would actually have been more pronounced); hence the reduced data base in "No. of situations" from 175 to 170 in the case of pairs and 165 in the case of triplets.

hunch, or method to go on. As its low number indicates, you should avoid it or ignore it entirely when any other indicator is present that would lend more than Rule 1's purely statistical validity.

As you can see clearly in Table II, more than half of the correct answers *will* actually fall under choice *a*, *c*, and *e*. Random probability suggests that each column *should* contain 20 percent of the correct answers. But since they don't, on any given guess the odds favor choice *b* and choice *d* over any *one* of the other three.

TABLE II 29

THE CORRELATION OF RULE 1 TO A TYPICAL REAL TEST COMPRISING 175 QUESTIONS

	No. of situations	No. of ans. by chance	No. of ans. by actual count	Variance between actual count and chance
Occurrences of *a*, *c*, or *e*	175	105	98	+7.1%
Occurrences of *c* only	175	35	27	+29.9%
Occurrences of pairs	170	34	21	+62.6%
Occurrences of pairs of *a*'s, *c*'s, or *e*'s	170	20.4	6	+242.9%
Occurrences of pairs of *c*'s only	170	6.8	(None)	∞!
Occurrences of triplets	165	6.6	3	+122.2%
Occurrences of triplets of *a*'s, *c*'s, or *e*'s	165	3.96	(None)	∞!
Occurrences of triplets of *c*'s only	165	1.32	(None)	∞!

EXAMPLES

1. xxxxxxxxxxxxxxxxxxxx?

(a) xxxxxxxxxx
(b) xxxxxxxxxx
(c) xxxxxxxxxx
(d) xxxxxxxxxx
(e) xxxxxxxxxx

As the x's above are meant to symbolize, you have drawn a complete blank on this question. It's as if the whole thing were written in Greek. Moreover, let us assume you have no information about the preceding or succeeding questions either.

This is the most extreme case of being in the dark you will ever encounter, and you will probably not encounter it frequently. Still, it is wise to venture a guess. You apply the Rule "Avoid Aces," and you are left with b or d to choose from. You guess either b or d—it doesn't much matter which, in theory—and you gain a slight statistical advantage over not guessing at all. (In this toss-up situation, I myself slightly favor b, but there is not enough statistical basis for urging this answer on you.)

2. xxxxxxxxxxxxxxxxxxxx?

(a) Eliminated
(b) xxxxxxxxxx
(c) xxxxxxxxxx
(d) Eliminated
(e) xxxxxxxxxx

You have eliminated a and d by your knowledge or other means (such as the presence of these answers in neighboring questions). Otherwise, the situation remains the same as in the previous example. You again apply the Rule "Avoid Ace," but this time you are left only with b. You guess b, and you gain a significantly greater (but still slight) advantage than on the previous example.

3. xxxxxxxxxxxxxxxxxxxx?

(a) xxxxxxxxxx
(b) Eliminated
(c) xxxxxxxxxx
(d) Eliminated
(e) xxxxxxxxxx

Same as previous example, except that b and d have been eliminated this time. You apply "Avoid Ace," but make no further progress thereby. So you remember to "Especially Avoid c," and are left with a good gambler's choice in a or e. You guess a or e—it doesn't matter which, in theory—and you gain a slight statistical edge over not guessing at all.

4. xxxxxxxxxxxxxxxxxxxx?

(a) xxxxxxxxxx
(b) Eliminated
(c) xxxxxxxxxx
(d) Eliminated
(e) Eliminated

Same as previous example, except that e has also been

eliminated. You apply the Rule "Avoid Aces, Especially *c*," and are left with a clear preference for *a*. You guess *a* and gain a significantly greater advantage than in the previous example.

5. xxxxxxxxxxxxxxxxxxxx?

(a) xxxxxxxxxx
(b) Eliminated
(c) Eliminated
(d) xxxxxxxxxx
(e) xxxxxxxxxx

(In addition, you are virtually certain that the correct answer to the previous question in this hypothetical situation is *d*, and that the correct answer to the succeeding question is *e*.)

Now you have a great deal of information, some of it conflicting. Avoiding *a*, *c*, *e*, you are left with only *d* to choose from. But avoiding pairs, you are left with only *a* to choose from. So, what to do?

You recall that the higher the Rule number, the more weight it has. And since the part of Rule 1 that advises you to avoid pairs follows and in effect has a higher Rule number (Rule 1, part 2) than the part that says avoid *a*, *c*, *e* (Rule 1, part 1), you avoid pairs and select *a*, the better bet. (The worst bet, apart from *b* and *c*, which you had already eliminated to your satisfaction, is *e* because there are *two* reasons not to pick it—avoiding *a*, *c*, *e*

and avoiding pairs.)

As you can see, a great deal of leeway in applying Rule 1 is given to your imagination and common sense. This will be equally true of subsequent Rules and of using Rules in combination.

Every situation will be different, and it is not possible or desirable to give a comprehensive game plan for all situations in this small space. Furthermore, as already stressed, nothing is ever guaranteed. Indeed, for the five examples just given, the *random* (wild guessing) odds are that you would average only one correct answer (20 percent). But, by applying my system of calculated guessing, you can expect to do better than 20 percent over the long haul— although you should not realistically expect to have gotten more than two of these five questions correct. That many would have been quite satisfactory, and any happy surprise of getting three or more correct would have been due as much to your good luck as to your good strategy. But Fortune does favor the bold.

PRACTICE QUESTIONS

All of these questions assume that you are in the bail-out stage, which is the most propitious time for exercising Rule 1.

1. Previous answer:
probably *a*.

Q: xxxxxxxxxxxxxxxxxx?

(a) xxxxxxxxxx
(b) xxxxxxxxxx
(c) xxxxxxxxxx
(d) xxxxxxxxxx
(e) xxxxxxxxxx

Following answer:
definitely *d*.

Avoiding Aces and the pairs *aa* and *dd*, you are left with only a reasonable guess at *b*. There's no guarantee, but by answering *b* you will gain a slight statistical edge.

2. Previous answer:
definitely *b*.

Q: xxxxxxxxxxxxxxxxxx?

(a) xxxxxxxxxx
(b) Eliminated
(c) xxxxxxxxxx
(d) Eliminated
(e) xxxxxxxxxx

Following answer: no idea yet; haven't attempted it.

If time permits, first try solving the subsequent question in the test in order to gain some more information about pairs to avoid. If that fails or if there isn't enough time, the Rule about avoiding *c* even more than *a* and *e* still leaves you the choice of either *a* or *e*. It's a toss-up, but be sure to guess one or the other and not leave the question unanswered.

3. Previous two answers:
probably *b*.

Q. xxxxxxxxxxxxxxxxxx?

(a) Eliminated
(b) xxxxxxxxxx
(c) xxxxxxxxxx
(d) Eliminated
(e) Eliminated

Following two answers:
definitely *c*.

Whether you guess *b* or *c*, you are headed into a triplet. (And they do occur, though infrequently.) But *b* is the better answer here both because *ccc* should be avoided on the basis of both parts of Rule 1 and because you are yourself less sure of the previous *bb* sequence. If either of these previous *b*'s turns out to have been incorrect, your double jeopardy of a triplet fore and aft vanishes.

4. Previous answer: *d*.

Q: xxxxxxxxxxxxxxxxxx?

(a) Eliminated
(b) Eliminated
(c) xxxxxxxxxx
(d) xxxxxxxxxx
(e) Eliminated

Following answer: *d*.

Since Part 2 of Rule 1 (Avoid Pairs and Triplets) takes precedence over Part 1 (Avoid Ace) owing to its higher number, clearly your best bet is to pick answer *c*. Even though *c* comes up a winner less frequently than it "should," it still comes up a great deal of the time. Triplets, on the other hand, come up far less frequently than single *c*'s. None of the Rules should ever be viewed as rigid prohibitions if the circumstances warrant flexibility.

5. Previous two answers: probably *c*.

Q: xxxxxxxxxxxxxxxxxxx?

(a) Probably eliminated
(b) Probably eliminated
(c) xxxxxxxxxx
(d) Probably eliminated
(e) Probably eliminated

Following two answers: probably *c*.

This is an extreme situation. It's possible but highly unlikely that there would ever be five correct *c*'s in a row. But because each question must be first approached *on its own merits*, the only sane answer is *c*. So select *c* by all means, but if you have time after you've filled in all the other answers, return to these five questions to make sure you haven't made a mistake in one or more of them.

And remember, in general, that as long as you have any reasonable grounds for giving a particular answer, don't change it for a less compelling one.

RULE

2

GENERAL
RULE

AVOID NON-ANSWERS

Avoid "None of the above," "It cannot be determined," and all other non-answer answers.

WHY THIS RULE WORKS

The "Non-Answer" answer, of which two common examples are given in the Rule formulation above, is found in great abundance on most multiple-choice tests. There are two reasons for its frequent use, and both of them point to an inherent vulnerability in questions that contain it.

The first reason why test makers like to use it is an aggressive one: The non-answer is a deceptive ploy, a loaded question, calculated to trap the diffident and the lame. The test maker theorizes that you may well be able to eliminate one or two of the five answer choices, that you will then be inclined to guess from among the three or four remaining choices, and that you will take the bait by figuring: "If the answer is clearly not one or two of the above, then it stands a good chance of being none of the above." That's where you will be most likely to go wrong.

The second reason the test maker resorts to the non-answer is a defensive one: he sometimes finds it difficult to think up five equally plausible answer choices, so rather than include an obvious red herring, he opts for a less visible red herring—the non-answer. Again, it is worth noting, he *intentionally* includes it as a wrong answer.

Of course, just to offset his own potential vulnerability should this ploy ever become widely known, he occasionally inserts a question which *is* correctly answered "none of the above," but since this type of question is difficult to create convincingly and tends to be a poor question type anyway, he inserts far fewer of them than he should to totally even things out. So the bottom line is: In a guessing situation, although you can't be absolutely sure that a non-answer is the wrong answer, it is wrong *enough of the time* to make it a bad choice for a wild guess and a good choice only when you have definitely eliminated *all* other choices.

I tested this Rule on a number of real examinations of various types. I found that the results supported this Rule convincingly. The analysis of one typical exam is shown in Table III (page 37). There was a total of 58 questions to which this Rule could be applied.

HOW AND WHEN TO USE THIS RULE

Non-answers announce themselves. You will not even have to be reminded of this Rule when you see a non-answer. They may appear as "None of the above," "It cannot be determined (from the information given)," "No error" (in questions where four other choices are given for correcting an error in the wording of the question), and so on.*

By nature, non-answers almost always appear in column *e*, as the last choice, a fact which coincidentally makes this Rule easy to use in conjunction with Rule 1 (Avoid Aces).

Non-answers sometimes appear in the same question as "super-answers" such as "All of the above" or "All are true." (Super-answers are actually a special subclass of non-answers.) A typical sequence containing both might go something like this:

Q: Which of the following are smaller than a bread box?

(a) Protons
(b) Neutrons
(c) Electrons
(d) All of the above
(e) None of the above

And sometimes super-answers appear unaccompanied by their negative twin:

Q: Which of the following are smaller than a bread box?

(a) Protons
(b) Neutrons
(c) Electrons
(d) Atoms
(e) All of the above

---

*In mathematical questions the answers 0 and 1 sometimes but not always function as non-answers. Mention of this is made in Rule 5 (page 51).

HOW TO READ THIS TABLE

The table assumes (unrealistically) that the test taker was not able to positively ascertain any of the eleven *correct* non-answers. In real life he or she would have solved many if not all of them from his or her knowledge alone, leaving a considerably higher and perhaps astronomically higher guessing edge than 14.5 percent on those questions that remained to be guessed at. For example, eliminating even three correct non-answers by virtue of having sniffed them out raises the guessing edge to 57.5 percent.

In either case, the same Rule holds for super-answers as for the negative form of non-answer: Never *guess* that they are correct. However, common sense dictates that if you know that two or more of the answer choices appearing with a super-answer are both equally correct, then you can be sure that the correct answer to the question will be the super-answer. Thus, if you knew beyond doubt in either of the above examples that protons and neutrons *at least* are smaller than a bread box, you should, of course, answer "All of the above."

THE CORRELATION OF RULE 2 TO A TYPICAL REAL TEST

	Number of situations	Number of correct non-answers by pure chance	Number of correct non-answers by actual count	Variance between actual count and chance
Questions having 5 answer choices	38	7.6	7	+8.7%
Questions having 4 answer choices	20	5	4	+25%
Average		12.6	11	+14.5%

No matter how tempting, never guess wildly in favor of a non-answer choice. On the contrary, if there is any doubt in your mind, eliminate the non-answer from contention and guess from among only the answers that remain. The non-answer should only be chosen if you have a lock on it; that is, only if you have satisfied yourself that all other answers are clearly wrong. For example:

Q: Which of the following are smaller than a bread box?

(a) Setafors
(b) Frammises
(c) Trippetarians
(d) All of the above
(e) None of the above

Even if you had no idea as to the meaning of a, b, and c words (they are actually nonsense words that could never appear on a real test), guess in favor of any of them sooner than choosing answer d or e.

EXAMPLES

1. Which of the following newspapers is published in New York?

(a) The New York Times
(b) The Washington Post
(c) The Philadelphia Enquirer
(d) All of the above
(e) None of the above

First, imagine that even though

you live in Rangoon, you *know* that *The New York Times*, at least, is correct, but you are not sure whether *b* and *c* are red herrings. You could safely eliminate choice *e* but you might be inclined to guess *d*. Don't! In such circumstances it is far better to pick a single sure answer than a non-answer which introduces one or more new elements of uncertainty.

Second, let's now imagine that you are equally unsure about all three newspapers. In this case, there is still no good reason to guess at answers *d* or *e*. It would be a statistically better guess to pick randomly from among *a*, *b*, and *c*. And it should again be stressed that to take full advantage of this system, you *must* make such a guess rather than leave the question unanswered.

Of course, with the advantage of the knowledge that you actually have about this silly question, you may be led to think that this advice is reckless. After all, the answer is *a*. And the odds are no better than one in three that you would guess the right answer by following this advice—even if *d* and *e* didn't exist as choices (and let's not forget that they do). But if you were truly in the dark, you would actually be *improving* your odds by guessing *a*, *b*, or *c*, not *decreasing* them, since the statistical probability against a correct non-answer or

super-answer makes the remaining choices the favorites.

2. Which of the following are animals?

(a) Trees
(b) Tomatoes
(c) Rocks
(d) Spoons
(e) None of the above

First, let's imagine that through your knowledge you are able to positively ascertain that none of the four choices— trees, tomatoes, rocks, spoons— are animals. The answer boils down to "None of the above." This is a very different type of situation than a guessing game and is the only situation in which you should select "none of the above."

A more likely situation, however, would be one in which some uncertainty exists. So imagine two more questions like the foregoing, but in which choice *d* has been replaced with a more obscure term:

2a. Which are animals?

(a) Trees
(b) Tomatoes
(c) Rocks
(d) Ais
(e) None of the above

2b. Which are animals?

(a) Trees
(b) Tomatoes
(c) Rocks
(d) Aix
(e) None of the above

Forget for the moment—if you

happen to know these words—that ais are South American three-toed tree sloths and Aix is a town in the south of France. In either case, statistical probability dictates that you *not* pick *e* (None of the above) even though in your certain elimination of choices *a*, *b*, and *c* you are already three-quarters of the way to that conclusion. Rather, pick *d*. In one case you'll turn out to be right and in the other you'll be wrong, but your cumulative performance on the test as a whole, assuming many other questions of this type, will benefit from this strategy.

PRACTICE QUESTIONS

1. If $\frac{1}{8}$ of a number is 3, what is $\frac{1}{3}$ of the number?

(a) 24
(b) 8
(c) 3
(d) 1
(e) It cannot be determined from the information given

This is an actual question from an SAT exam. Presumably, through algebra or trial-and-error, you will be able to solve it. But let's imagine you could not solve it. Your strategy would then be to avoid the non-answer and guess from among *a*, *b*, *c*, and *d*. Perhaps other help would be present in a real test, such as the previous and following answers (see Rule 1, part 2),

but if not, you would give a slight preference to answers *b* and *d* (Rule 1, part 1), and then give it the old eeny, meeny, miney, mo. (The correct answer, by the way, is *b*.)

2. Directions: The following sentence contains a problem in grammar, usage, diction, or idiom. It *may* be correct or it may contain an error. The error, if there is one, is underlined and lettered. Assume that all other elements of the sentence are correct and cannot be changed. Select the one underlined part that must be changed in order to make the sentence correct, or if there is no error, select answer *e*.

Q: While modernizing the fac-
        (a)
tory, the company ran out of
                    (b)
money and must secure a loan
            (c)
so that it could finish buying
                    (d)
the new equipment. No error.
                        (e)

This is also an actual question from an SAT exam. Presumably your knowledge of grammar will lead you to the correct answer, which was arrived at by 80 percent of the test takers. But let's imagine that you could not solve it. Your strategy would then be to avoid the non-answer and guess from among *a*, *b*, *c*, and *d*. Especially if you were able to ascertain that *a*, *b*, and *d* contain perfectly natural English, but couldn't quite be sure whether the error occurs at *c* or not at all, it would be a substantially better risk to guess *c* than to guess *e*. In fact, the error (the correct answer) does occur at *c*, which should read "and had to."

3. Directions: This question consists of two quantities, one in column A and one in column B. You are to compare the two quantities and select your answer as follows:

(a) If the quantity in column A is greater

(b) If the quantity in column B is greater

(c) If the two quantities are equal

(d) If the relationship cannot be determined from the information given

(e) Does not appear at all as a choice in this kind of question.

Q: On a certain day, 80 percent of the girls and 75 percent of the boys were present in a mathematics class.

Column A	Column B
The no. of girls absent	The no. of boys absent

Again, an actual question from an SAT test. If you found yourself completely in the dark on this question, you might have been led by Rule 2 to reject choice *d* and guess from among *a*, *b*, and *c*. But this is one case where you would have been dead wrong by applying my strategy, because the correct answer is *d*. Frankly there's no helping it. And I have inten-

tionally included some examples like this one in which my strategy fails so you won't acquire any illusions about it.

But look again. This is precisely the kind of poorly constructed and rather obvious question I mentioned earlier that is thrown in to maintain the credibility of the non-answer column. The least bit of effort made toward understanding the question reveals it for what it is. So, as with all questions, it must be assumed that you will make a serious effort to solve it and thereby minimize the chance that the system will backfire on any given question. When you realize, in this case, that you are not told how many boys or girls are enrolled in the class, you also realize that you could never know, based on percentages alone, which of the two groups had more absentees. The inanity of the question becomes obvious, as is often the case when a non-answer turns out to be the correct answer.

■■■■■■

RULE 3

STANDARD
MULTIPLE-CHOICE
QUESTION

STAY CLOSE TO THE CENTER OF SYM-METRY

When all five answer choices form a series such as 2, 3, 4, 5, 6, stay close to the center (of numerical symmetry). Avoid the two extremes.

MEMORY AID:

Center of Symmetry

WHY THIS RULE WORKS

The multiple-choice format makes tests easy, fast, and inexpensive to correct and grade. It achieves this objective by leaving nothing to the grader's or the grading machine's imagination. But everything has its price, and the test is thereby left with a built-in weakness: It needs "smoke screens" to make it work effectively.

Accordingly, one of the test maker's most important functions—in a way even more important to his success than dreaming up good questions to ask—is *hiding the correct answer well.* He accomplishes this by carefully selecting and arranging the *wrong* answers in such a way as to make the right answer "invisible."

In other words, he camouflages or "smoke-screens" it. But a trained eye can see through it. Indeed the very presence and nature of the smoke can tell you a great deal.

The test maker knows that the best diversionary tactics are the most plausible ones. Thus, especially in mathematical problems, he often hides the correct answer by sandwiching it between two or more of its near neighbors.

For example, if the correct answer to a given problem is 7, and it's pretty obvious from the question that the answer must in any case be a low whole number, his ideal tactic would be to hide it among 5, 6, 8, and 9.

Of course, he realizes that what is ideal in one sense may leave him especially vulnerable to precisely the kind of induction we are making here, so he varies his tactic a little, say by changing the range of answer choices to 5, 6, 7, 9, and 10; or 6, 7, 8, 9, and 10; or 3, 5, 6, 7, and 9; or some other such minor variant.

But, for a very good reason, he rarely leaves the correct answer "exposed" at either end of the series (in columns *a* or *e*), as for example by the series 7, 8, 9, 10, 11; or 2, 3, 5, 6, 7. The reason is that he knows that a "buried" answer has twice as much potential to fool you as an exposed answer. This is true because if an answer is sandwiched between other, similar numbers, you stand half a chance of erring by overcalculating and half a chance by undercalculating the correct answer.

But if an answer is exposed at either end of a series, one of these two chances for falling on your face has been eliminated. And since the test maker *needs* every edge he can get to make sure that a substantial number of people do fall on their faces, he has a vested interest in making sandwiches. Hence, when all five answer choices form a neat and regular (or nearly regular) series, stay close to the center of numerical symmetry.

You will note that I have not said "stay *at* the center" but simply "stay close to" it. The reason for this flexibility is that, as already mentioned, the test maker tends to avoid regular use of precise symmetry because of the help this would presumably give to wild guessers.

Therefore, it turns out that there is a slightly higher probability that the answer will fall *to either side* of the center of symmetry rather than directly on the center, that is, in columns *b* and *d*, rather than predominantly in column *c*. This fact makes it easy to use Rule 3 in conjunction with Rule 1 (Avoid Aces), provided you don't rule out column *c* entirely.

Of the forty multiple-choice math questions that appear on the test given in *Taking the SAT*, eleven had answer choices that consisted of a regular or nearly regular sequence of whole numbers. Of these eleven, none had column *a* as the correct answer, and only one had column *e*. (This latter was the predictable and necessary "giveaway" question answered correctly by 91 percent of all test takers.) Seven of the eleven correct answers fell in columns *b* and *d* and only three in column *c*.

HOW AND WHEN TO USE THIS RULE

Adopt the "Center of Symmetry" Rule whenever the answer choices even remotely resemble a neat and orderly sequence of numbers. In such a situation, all other things being equally uncertain, the best *guesses* are *b* and *d*, with *c* a close third—in some tests I have analyzed, *c*'s equal or outnumber *b*'s or *d*'s. It is definitely better to guess *b*, *c*, or *d* than not to guess at all.

The Rule applies particularly well to simple numerical series (such as 9, 10, 11, 12, 13) and arithmetical sequences (7, 14, 21, 28, 35); it applies less well *but still applies* to geometrical sequences (1, 3, 9, 27, 81), fractional progressions ($\frac{3}{7}, \frac{4}{7}, \frac{5}{7}, \frac{6}{7}$, 1), and uneven progressions (32, 36, 40, 48, 64). But the Rule should be totally abandoned when there appears to be no rhyme or reason for connecting the several answer choices to one another ($\frac{1}{2}, \frac{6}{13}, \frac{5}{13}, \frac{3}{10}, \frac{3}{13}$ or 0, 1, 2, 3, 128).

EXAMPLE

How many surfaces are there on a cube?

(a) 4
(b) 6
(c) 7
(d) 8
(e) 10

First, imagine that you really don't know the correct answer and haven't a clue. You do, however, recognize in the sequence 4, 6, 7, 8, 10 a thinly disguised Rule 3 situation. You rule out a and e, and are left with b, c, and d to choose from. (In this situation, there is not yet any strong reason to favor b or d over c, so you do not rule out c.) You look for other clues such as the answers to neighboring questions (Rule 1: Avoid Pairs), and if none are available, you simply close your eyes, apply the other part of Rule 1 to the bcd choice (Avoid Ace), and therefore pick b or d. Of course, the correct answer is b, and in creating this example to support the Rule, I may be accused of loading the deck, but I will be giving "equal time" to a situation that violates the Rule in one of the practice questions below.

PRACTICE QUESTIONS

1. xxxxxxxxxxxxxxxxxxxx?

(a) 75
(b) 150
(c) 225
(d) 300
(e) 375

You draw a blank on the question, you recognize the numerical series, and you stay close to the center of symmetry, selecting an answer from among b, d, and c. If the answers to neighboring questions were available, you would of course consult them to avoid pairs (Rule 1). That is about all that can be squeezed out of this situation, but that is at least something.

2. If x and y are positive integers and $x - y = 5$, what is the least possible value of $x + y$?

(a) 6
(b) 7
(c) 8
(d) 9
(e) 10

This is an actual question from an SAT exam. Only 52 percent of all the test takers got it right. If everyone had applied Rules 3 and 1 alone, 50 percent would presumably have guessed b and 50 percent d. And 50 percent would have gotten it right (even without reading the question!) because the correct answer is b.

3. If $x = 3$, then $x^2 + 3 =$ ___.

(a) 0
(b) 3
(c) 6
(d) 9
(e) 12

This is another actual question from an SAT exam. But in this case 91 percent of all test takers got it right. If they had all applied Rule 3, *none* would have gotten it right, because the correct answer is e! Chalk up one defeat for Rule 3.

But look again. This question is a clear giveaway even for

grade school students. It is a question for which no guessing Rules are necessary. Its sole purpose is to give choice *e* some credibility and incidentally to separate the somewhat lame goats from the extremely lame goats. But since you will be using your knowledge before resorting to wild guesses, you are actually a lot safer from the bite of the outside columns than even my statistical analysis indicates (one chance in eleven).

RULE 4

STANDARD
MULTIPLE-CHOICE
QUESTION

GO FOR BROKE (ALMOST)

When you are asked for the smallest number of things that meet a certain condition or criterion, select the smallest or *next-to-smallest* of the answer choices; when you are asked for the greatest number, select the greatest or *next-to-greatest* answer.

WHY THIS RULE WORKS

This Rule is, paradoxically, both an exception to and a corroboration of Rule 3 (Center of Symmetry). The same motive that the test maker has for sandwiching a correct answer between other plausible answers (Rule 3) leads him to behave slightly differently, but predictably, in creating the smoke screen for questions that ask for an *extreme*.

For example, one such question might read: What is the smallest number of dimes you could ever receive in change when tendering a dollar to a cashier for a purchase? Or, what is the greatest number of dimes in such a situation? In this case, he uses his smoke to work up to (or down to) the correct answer with as long a series of numbers as seems plausible.

He imagines you, the typical test taker, being able to recall or imagine having on various real-life occasions received four, five, or even six dimes in change when making a purchase with a dollar bill. His best test of your ingenuity is rightly viewed by him as beginning somewhere *far short of* the right answer and progressing toward the target, but not significantly beyond.

So, if you've gotten four dimes on occasion, is it possible that you could get as few as three, two, one or even no dimes at all on some other occasion? And having once gotten six dimes, is there a situation when you might actually receive seven, eight, nine, or ten dimes in change from your purchase? The test maker naturally spreads his smoke *toward* the actual answer, and perhaps slightly beyond, just to keep you honest. Accordingly, in asking for the smallest possible number of dimes you could receive (the answer is *none*), he might structure his choices as follows:

(a) 4
(b) 3
(c) 2
(d) 1
(e) 0

And in asking for the largest possible number of dimes (and let's assume the answer is 9, after the cost of your purchase has been subtracted from your dollar) he might structure his answer choices as follows:

(a) 10
(b) 9
(c) 8
(d) 7
(e) 6

But when asking for the largest number he would be *very unlikely* to structure the answers thus:

(a) 17
(b) 14
(c) 13
(d) 11
(e) 9

It's easy to see why. In the case of extreme questions, he is not so interested in making a good sandwich as in forcing you to dig your way *in* toward the meat. Any answers appreciably beyond the correct answer are, in his strategy, wasted as smoke. Thus his smoke screen must be lopsided, with all or nearly all of the smoke concentrated on the near side of the target.

HOW AND WHEN TO USE THIS RULE

The telltale words for identifying situations when Rule 4 will be useful are "greatest," "most," "maximum," "largest"; and conversely, "least," "fewest," "minimum," "smallest." It's that simple. These words will actually appear in the question and by their presence will remind you to "Go for Broke (Almost)."

In situations where this Rule overlaps with its opposite and twin, Rule 3, you will have an even more favorable guessing edge. If you combine "Stay Close to the Center of Symmetry" (i.e., *bcd*) with "Go for Broke (Almost)" (i.e., *ab* or *de*, depending on direction), you will be left with a single best bet in every case. A situation in which these two Rules apply simultaneously is as close to a dead giveaway as you will ever find in a test question. In the SAT exam I have been citing, there were four occurrences of this happy situation, and three of them were correctly answered by the next-to-extreme choice. (The fourth occurrence was correctly answered by *c* and had a complicating factor that will be described below in practice question 2, but I include it in the analysis here so as to be statistically fair.) That's three out of four hits when the random odds called for .8 out of four: a 275 percent gambling edge!

If you will look *back* to practice question 2 under Rule 3 (page 44), you will perhaps be surprised to realize that we have already examined just such a Rule-3-and-4 situation. But when you notice the presence of the word "least" in that question, you will not be surprised that the answer is *b*.

EXAMPLE

What is the *greatest* number of equilateral triangular pieces of paper with sides of length 2 and altitude of length $\sqrt{3}$ that can be cut whole from a rectangular sheet of paper with dimensions 6 by $\sqrt{3}$?

(a) 7
(b) 5
(c) 4
(d) 3
(e) 2

This, too, is an actual question from an SAT exam, though the italics are mine. It is astonishing that fewer than 20 percent of the test takers got the correct answer. But you, immediately noticing the word "greatest" and the more or less orderly progression of answer choices, will automatically think of Rules 3 and 4, and will conclude that since Rule 3 strongly suggests a center of symmetry at bcd and Rule 4 suggests the extreme answers at ab, you have an odds-on favorite at the point of consensus in choice b. The answer *is*, again, b. I have not loaded the deck. Of the real questions at my disposal from the mentioned publication, there is only one that fails to follow form.

PRACTICE QUESTIONS

1. If the nine regions in the accompanying figure are to be colored so that no two bordering regions have the same color, what is the least number of colors that can be used?

(a) 2
(b) 3
(c) 4
(d) 5
(e) 6

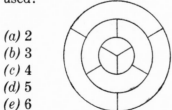

You may or may not have been able to solve this question by mathematical means (65 per-cent of all test takers got the right answer), but you can see that this is another occasion for applying both Rule 3 and Rule 4 to arrive at a preferred (correct) guess of b.

2. *Annual Swim Meet*

School	Back Stroke	Side Stroke	Crawl	Total
JEFFERSON				7
LINCOLN				9
WASHINGTON				

The table above shows the scorecard for a swim meet in which there were three races and no ties. In each race, points were awarded as follows: 5 points for first place, 3 points for second place, and 1 point for third place. What is the *greatest* number of third places that Lincoln could have taken?

(a) 3
(b) 2
(c) 1
(d) 0
(e) It cannot be determined from the information given

I have included this question as fair warning against jumping to conclusions even on the combined strength of all four of the Rules presented thus far. Rule 1 (Avoid Aces) tentatively argues in favor of b or d; Rule 2 (Avoid Non-Answers) prejudices you against e, at least, and perhaps also against d; Rule 3 (Center of Symmetry) seems to rule out a and d and lend its support to b and c; and

Rule 4 (Go for Broke, Almost) reaffirms *b*. Everything converges upon *b*. The correct answer, however, is *c*! So if you were unable to *solve* this problem (as were 53 percent of the test takers), you'd have been left guessing at a wrong answer.

There is no point hiding or minimizing the fact that on any given question the system may or may not work. But looking over my shoulder at this question (I frankly admit that it haunts me), I can see in retrospect *why* it does not hold true to form. In this case the test maker was limited by the very unusual nature of the question itself to precisely the five answer choices that actually appear, and no others. He had no freedom in the matter to strategize. The numbers *had* to be the integers from 0 to 3 and a nonanswer! Thus we can blame the arithmetical structure of the question for our losing the point rather than our opponent himself. Small comfort, but I mention it because the ability to see through this kind of phenomenon in a question is actually valuable. When you see a situation like this, suspend all the usual bets, because your tactics are no longer directed against the test maker but against Mother Nature. And with her you can only break even.

RULE 5

STANDARD
MULTIPLE-CHOICE
QUESTION

LOOK FOR THE NUCLEAR ANSWER

Choose the answer which contains the most elements held in common by the majority of the answer choices.

MEMORY AID:

Nuclear Answer

WHY THIS RULE WORKS

In problems involving computation, the test maker naturally constructs his smoke screen out of the incorrect answers which are most likely to arise from computational or conceptual errors. Since he is *trying* to misdirect you, it makes a great deal of sense, from his point of view, to give you all the rope you need to hang yourself. One slip of the pencil or of the mind, and you will come up with an incorrect answer that is all the more plausible because you find it among the answer choices. You say to yourself, "Eureka, I've got it," and he grinds you into the dust.

But what he does not realize is that this particular kind of smoke is especially easy to see through. Since every incorrect answer choice he supplies you with varies from the correct answer by one or more degrees of deviation, you stand a good chance of being able to reconstruct the correct answer with a little intelligent detective work. The key is to find the one answer from which all the near misses were generated.

For example, consider the five answer choices:

(a) 1.2
(b) 12
(c) 13
(d) 18
(e) 120

You can see, even without benefit of reading the question, that answers *abe* have in common the fact that they are decimal multiples of 1.2, and that answers *bcd* are all roughly the same order of magnitude. The one answer choice that appears in both of these subgroups is *b*. Armed with this deductive information, we can proceed to reconstruct the test maker's deception in more detail. Presumably he started with a correct answer of 12 that he wanted to hide and a problem involving two kinds of computation or reasoning: a decimal aspect and a numerical (or counting) aspect. He created two puffs of smoke for each, since he figured you were as likely to go astray on one aspect as on the other. Hence 1.2 and 120 are the decimal variants, and 13 and 18 the numerical variants, of the correct answer, 12.

In the test presented in *Taking the SAT*, of the forty multiple-choice math questions there were sixteen which showed signs of being solvable or partly solvable by this Rule. Of the eight in which I felt perfectly comfortable in pointing to a single and definite best guess by this Rule, six were indeed correct and only two were wrong—a 275 percent guessing edge over random probability. Of the eight others in which I felt comfortable only in eliminating certain of the answers from consideration but not in pointing to a single correct answer, I successfully eliminated sixteen answer choices in six questions, leaving on average 2.3 of the five original answer choices to guess from (see Table I, page 20, for the implications of this), and I was completely fooled on the two remaining questions—but still came out with a 72 percent guessing edge over random probability. Thus, in all I had 8.75 correct answers out of sixteen, when only 3.2 were to be expected, for an overall guessing edge of 172 percent *without even reading the question.* In actual raw score this represents a net gain of nearly seven correct answers or 60 to 70 extra points!

HOW AND WHEN TO USE THIS RULE

Whenever you see a choice of five apparently diverse and yet partially related answer choices, you have good reason to apply Rule 5. As mentioned, in a typical test with forty multiple-choice questions, this technique worked—fully or partially—for sixteen of them, so this is an important Rule, and one you will use frequently.

Whenever you see a device

TELLTALE SIGNS

The common factors which may relate answer choices are extremely varied and include:

- Decimal variations (3, 30, 300)
- Numerical (counting) variations (74, 75, 77)
- Fractional variations ($\frac{2}{7}$, $\frac{7}{3}$)
- Multiplicative variations (11, 22, 44, 88)
- Variations of exponent (a, a^2, a^3)
- Variations of a common term

$$(\frac{a-1}{2}, \frac{a}{a-1}, \frac{a-1}{a+1},$$

in which all three terms contain, in this case, "$a-1$")
- Variations of common divisor (12, 16, 20, 28)
- Variations on a function ($2\sqrt{3}$, $3\sqrt{2}$, $3\sqrt{3}$, in which all three terms contain, in this case, a radical sign)
- Variations on an operation ($k-j$, $j-k$, $k-l$, in which all three terms contain, in this case, a minus sign)

There are many other such "recurrent motifs," dictated by the particular question, but these should give you a good idea of what to expect.

repeated in some but not all of the answer choices, think "nuclear answer." You can apply the Rule by eliminating those answer choices that contain the fewest common motifs and, if a single preferred answer does not emerge outright, by guessing from among those which have the *most* common motifs. This may seem rather abstract, but the examples and practice questions that follow should bring it firmly down to earth for you.

EXAMPLES

1. In the accompanying figure, the area of the small square is x. If each short line segment in the figure has length 2y and every pair of intersecting segments is perpendicular, then the area of the shaded region in terms of x is

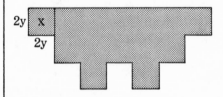

(a) 12x
(b) 13x
(c) 14x
(d) 14x²
(e) 196x²

This question comes from an actual SAT, as do all the other examples and practice questions concerning this Rule. Only

60 percent of all test takers got this one right, but it is a classic example of a Nuclear Answer giveaway. Ignore the question and the diagram, if you like. That is the beauty of Rule 5. (Of course on a real test you'd never ignore the question.) Examining the answer choices, you notice at first glance that they break down into three groups: *abc* (neighboring multiples of x), *cd* (fourteens), and *de* (related values of x²). Since the *abc* group is the largest and the most clearly defined, the answer will most likely be one of these. But additional information is provided by the presence of groups *cd* and *de*; items *c*, *d*, and *e* all involve the number 14 (or the square of 14), and all thus lend support to item *c*, which because it belongs both to the major group *and* to another group is therefore the odds-on favorite. In fact *c* is correct.

2. When purchased, a bottle with a 10-ounce capacity contains 8 ounces of soda. If the buyer drinks 6 ounces of the soda, then what percent of the bottle is empty?

(a) 20%
(b) 25%
(c) 60%
(d) 75%
(e) 80%

The answer choices here do not at first look too promising for application of Rule 5, but they actually are. What do you see?

Choices *ace* are all multiples of 20 while choices *bd* are multiples of 25. That already makes *ace* the favorites since they are in the majority. But of these three choices, only *c* does not have a "near neighbor"—in the sense that both *a* and *e* are accompanied at intervals of 5 percent by *b* and *d*, respectively. Therefore, since *a* and *e* have this additional feature in common, it is a fair bet to eliminate *c* from consideration.

In most examples of this type it is risky to press the issue any further than we already have, but it is tempting to note that in a situation of otherwise perfect balance, the value of *c* (60%) tilts the scale toward *de* and away from *ab*. (If the value of *c* had been 40%, the reverse would have been true.) Thus, faced with a choice between *a* and *e*, there is considerable but not compelling reason to favor *e*. (And *e* is correct.)

> **3.** How many cubes, each with surface area of 54 square centimeters, are needed to form 2 cubes, each with surface area of 216 square centimeters?
>
> (a) 4
> (b) 8
> (c) 10
> (d) 16
> (e) 32

I hasten to add this example directly on the heels of the previous one to point out how risky it can be to try to split hairs too finely. Fewer than 20 percent of the test takers got this one right. You would have been among the losers (as I was) if you had applied only Rule 5 and carried it to its sometimes overreaching conclusions. I reasoned: *abde* are all multiples of 4. Therefore rule out *c*. So far so good.

Then I decided to put *c* to some use in looking for an additional "motif." The value of *c* falls between *b* and *d*, and is in fact considerably closer to *b*. Therefore, I reasoned, guess *b*.

I went wrong (the correct answer is actually *d*) because I gave too much weight to too little information. In a case like this when motifs are not strongly developed in clusters of two and three about all you can safely assume is that the answer is probably *abde*, with a *slight* preference indicated for *bd*; but it would be a mistake to jump to any conclusions, even to entirely rule out *c*—the black sheep itself—since the fact remains that *all five* choices, by virtue of being even numbers, have a great deal in common. Here we are really as close to a Rule 3 (Center of Symmetry) situation as we are to a Rule 5, with neither one particularly well developed. Still, both Rules do argue in unison against choices *a* and *e* which boosts your guessing edge significantly.

4. If $\frac{7}{3}x = \frac{3}{7}y$ and $y \neq 0$,

then $\frac{x}{y} =$

(a) $\frac{9}{49}$

(b) $\frac{3}{7}$

(c) 1

(d) $\frac{7}{3}$

(e) $\frac{49}{9}$

Here is another problem that deserves caution. We can see the kinship of *ae* and also of *bd*; likewise the kinships of *ab* and of *de*. But we would be rash to rule out anything but *c*, since it alone is truly an odd man out. In the present case, answer *c* even has the distinct aura of a "Non-Answer" (Rule 2, see footnote, page 36) despite its seemingly "committed" appearance. But that's all one can safely say here, or the previous example taught us no lesson at all. The correct answer turns out to be *a*, and though Rule 5 should be commended for narrowing the answer choices by 20 percent to *abde*, it only goes that far here. Still, that's something.

5. If a is not 0 or 1, what is the

reciprocal of $\dfrac{a}{1 - \frac{1}{a}}$?

(a) $\dfrac{a-1}{a^2}$

(b) $\dfrac{a-1}{a}$

(c) a -1

(d) $\dfrac{1}{a-1}$

(e) $\dfrac{a^2}{a-1}$

Here the help provided by Rule 5 is more substantial and often saves the day in what may otherwise seem a hopeless situation. We can see that choices *ae* are reciprocals of one another, as are *cd*. (In dealing with a mix of whole numbers and fractions, it is sometimes helpful to express a whole number as "itself over 1"; thus *c* can be expressed as

$$\frac{a-1}{1}$$

making it the reciprocal of *d*—

$$\frac{1}{a-1} \cdot)$$

Therefore *b* (with no reciprocal) is an odd man out, leaving for the moment *acde*. But *b* itself reveals two additional puffs of smoke. It contains "a − 1" on the *top* side of the fraction, thus lending weight to the motif group *abc*, and it contains a second occurrence of the term "a," lending a bit more credence to *ae* (which also contain a second "a") than to *cd* (which do not). In addition, since *c* is not actually expressed as a fraction, it has less in common with the other answers than does *a*. All in all, these accumulated slight preferences for *a* make *a* a pretty good bet. And the answer is actually *a*.

PRACTICE QUESTIONS

1. If the average of v and w is p and the average of x, y, and z is q, what is the average of v, w, x, y, and z in terms of p and q?

(a) $p + q$

(b) $\dfrac{p + q}{2}$

(c) $2p + 3q$

(d) $\dfrac{2p + 3q}{5}$

(e) $\dfrac{3p + 2q}{5}$

Did you notice that *bde* are all fractions? Did you notice that *d* and *e* both have a denominator of 5? And did you notice that the numerator of *d* appears identically elsewhere (in *c*), while the numerator of *e* has no echo in any other answer? If so, you probably found the correct answer, *d*, with ease.

2. If the ratio of p to q is $\dfrac{3}{5}$ and the ratio of q to r is $\dfrac{10}{13}$, then the ratio of p to r is

(a) $\dfrac{1}{2}$

(b) $\dfrac{6}{13}$

(c) $\dfrac{5}{13}$

(d) $\dfrac{3}{10}$

(e) $\dfrac{3}{13}$

Did you notice that *bce* all have a denominator of 13? And did you notice that *d* and *e* both have a numerator of 3? If so, you probably *bungled*—as I did—into a wrong guess of *e*. (The correct answer, as it happens, is *b*.)

This question is one of the two I was virtually sure I had correct in the experimental analysis mentioned above. And this kind of occasional error is inevitable even with so powerful a Rule as Rule 5. I have no interest in hiding my failures from you; you must be fully apprised of the risks you will be taking with my system. Of course, in testing this Rule, I never even bothered to look at the question—and probably you didn't, either. We would not have been so blasé on a real test!

3. If the pyramid in the accompanying figure has a square base and all equilateral faces with edges of length 6, what is the perpendicular height of the pyramid?

(a) 3
(b) $2\sqrt{3}$
(c) $3\sqrt{2}$
(d) $3\sqrt{3}$
(e) 6

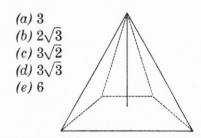

Did you notice that *bcd* all contain a radical? And that *b* and *c* both contain a 2 and a 3? If so, good.

Did you then decide that no further conclusions could be drawn with any increased hope of success? And did you then settle for a wild guess from between answers *b* and *c*? That's really all you can do in a case like this. But it *is* significant.

3a. Previous answer: *d*
Q: Same as question 3
Following answer: *b*

Were you reminded of Rule 1 (Avoid Pairs)? The existence of the neighboring answers *b* and *d* makes the choice between *b* and *c* no longer a toss-up but an easy choice in favor of *c*. The correct answer is *c*.

4. The accompanying figure shows a rod with black beads and white beads. How many beads must be slid from the right side to the left so that one-fourth of the beads on each side are black?

LEFT   RIGHT

(a) 2
(b) 4
(c) 5
(d) 6
(e) 9

Did you notice that *bcd* are near neighbors? Did you notice that *b* and *d* both have accompanying "smoke" (in *a* and *e* respectively, insofar as 2 has a common divisor with 4 as does 9 with 6)? Did you notice that *abd* are even numbers and there are elements of Center of Symmetry

(page 41) present? If so, good.

Did you then decide that no further conclusions could be drawn with any increased hope of success? And did you then settle for a wild guess from between answers *b* and *d*? Again, that is really all you can do here with this Rule. (Of course, we are intentionally overlooking the fact that this question is quite easy to solve directly.)

4a. Previous answer: *b*
Q: Same as question 4
Following answer: *b*

Now the situation is even more promising than it was in practice question 3a, above. The odds against three answers of the same letter in a row are so high that the choice of *d* here is a very good bet indeed. The correct answer is *d*.

5. Previous answer: *e*

Q: If $\frac{2}{3} \times \frac{3}{4} \times \frac{4}{5} \times \frac{5}{6} \times \frac{6}{7} \times y = 1$, then y =

(a) $\frac{2}{7}$

(b) 1

(c) 2

(d) $\frac{7}{2}$

(e) 7

Following answer: *b*

Did you notice that *a* and *d* are closely related, and not simply because they are both fractions?

(And that there are echoes of each of them in both c and e as well?) If so, good. The best guesses are a and d, and there is no help from the neighbors this time. A toss-up. (The correct answer is d.)

But if you reasoned that bce actually have more in common than ad because they are all whole numbers; that ce have just as much of an echo in ad as ad have in ce, and that the previous answer e makes c the best choice, you would have gone astray—for the following reasons:

1. By ascribing too much importance to the answer "1" (as noted before, it is often merely a non-answer, see page 34).

2. By failing to see that the presence of ce *follows from ad* and not vice versa (since both a and d *completely contain c and e* within them).

Your final conclusion in preferring c to e was absolutely reasonable but, since you had already gone astray, to no avail.

Admittedly, this is one instance (a rare one) where applying a Rule correctly is nearly as difficult as solving the test question itself. This may lead some readers to wonder whether my system isn't too unwieldy to be practical. But I think you will agree that any tool is better than no tool at all. If you had drawn a blank on this question and had time left for guessing, I daresay you'd have been grateful for this tool. Fully 46 percent of the test takers got this problem wrong.

On the other hand, if you ever find yourself fussing and getting upset over how to apply a Rule, just drop it. Leave the question unanswered or take a totally wild guess. If my system were ever to become an encumbrance to you, it would cease to be of any use because your first need is to remain free for dealing with the test on its own terms.

RULE 6

STANDARD
MULTIPLE-CHOICE
QUESTION

AVOID THE MONSTER

When four relatively simple answer choices appear together with a very large or complex fifth choice, avoid the latter.

WHY THIS RULE WORKS

This Rule is actually a logical extension of Rule 5. The test maker's penchant for creating his smoke screen out of wrong answers that might easily be reached through miscalculation leaves him especially vulnerable in cases where the miscalculation produces an unusually large or complex number. On most tests the questions are designed to require a minimum of time-consuming calculation, so the correct answers tend to be simple answers. The very presence of a monster among simple answers usually belies smoke.

HOW AND WHEN TO USE THIS RULE

Though it hardly seems profitable to digest an entire Rule for the occasional opportunity it affords of eliminating a single answer choice, this Rule often combines nicely with Rules 3 (Center of Symmetry) and 5 (Nuclear Answer). But even in those cases where no additional information can be gleaned (which are rare, considering that Rule 1 is almost always at your disposal), eliminating the monster and working with the four simpler answers will still give you a statistical edge of six extra correct answers per hundred (see Table I on page 20), an edge that would net you a bonus of more than 30 points on a typical math SAT.

As the name suggests, it is not difficult to recognize a monster. Any three-digit number among one-digit numbers, for example, or a wild-looking fraction among the garden variety fractions found on a measuring cup, or a long and precise decimal fraction among simpler numbers qualifies as a monster. A monster is not necessarily defined by its size alone but by its relationship to the other answer choices. Thus in the sequence 3, 6, 9, 12, 886, the last number is a monster. But 886 would not be a monster if it appeared in company with 4.43, 8.86, 44.3, and 88.6.

EXAMPLES

1. Which gives milk?

(a) Cow
(b) Bull
(c) Steer
(d) Chicken
(e) Tyrannosaurus rex

As you can see from this irreverent example (which, incidentally, is *not* a question type that appears on the SAT, though it does appear on many other tests), finding a monster is a little like playing the odd-man-out game. The point is, regardless of what the question is asking for, you should ask yourself, "Which of these creatures does not belong in this barnyard? I may not know which one gives the milk but I'll be damned if I guess Tyrannosaurus rex."

2. xxxxxxxxxxxxxxxxxxxxx?

(a) 3
(b) 9
(c) 27
(d) 81
(e) 243

2a. xxxxxxxxxxxxxxxxxxx?

(a) 1
(b) 2
(c) 4
(d) 8
(e) 243

In the case of example 2, the number 243, though it may look surprising, is *not* a monster because it is a natural outgrowth of the series, which in this case grows by multiples of 3. But in example 2a, the number 243 *is* a monster because it stands in no apparent relationship to the other answers.

3. xxxxxxxxxxxxxxxxxxxx?

(a) $\frac{1}{2}$
(b) 2
(c) 4
(d) 6
(e) 8

A borderline case, but $\frac{1}{2}$ is probably a monster. There is some doubt, however, because

even though $\frac{1}{2}$ is very different from the other answers, it is not a very complex number, and it actually differs from one of the other answer choices, *b*, by no greater a factor than *b* differs from *e* (i.e., 4×). An ideal monster is both very remote from and very much more complex than the other answer choices.

4. $\left(\frac{2}{3} \div \frac{3}{4} \right) - \left(\frac{1}{9} \div \frac{1}{7} \right) =$

(a) $\frac{-9}{56}$

(b) 0

(c) $\frac{1}{9}$

(d) $\frac{335}{630}$

(e) $\frac{8}{7}$

This is a real question from the SAT. You may well have been suspicious of answer *d* and probably also of *a* since it too has borderline-monster qualities *and* is the only answer choice with a minus sign. That already narrows the field, but if you take Rule 5 (Nuclear Answer) into account, answer *b* also becomes unlikely since it is a zero surrounded by four fractions (and appearing in this context has the odor of a nonanswer as well, see footnote on page 36). Also keeping Rule 5 in mind, of the two remaining choices, only *c* has an echo elsewhere (in the 9 that appears in choice *a*), and is therefore a *slight* favorite. We cannot be too sure of ourselves in this case because the process of deduction that led us to this answer was fairly roundabout. But if no other route is available, a roundabout approach based on a loose interpretation of the Rules, though less reliable, should definitely be attempted. In actual fact, the correct answer is *c*, and in this instance we can congratulate ourselves as much for our luck as for our method.

PRACTICE QUESTIONS

1. xxxxxxxxxxxxxxxxxxxxx?

(a) 12x
(b) 13x
(c) 14x
(d) 14x^2
(e) 196x^2

Choice *e* is borderline—not very clear-cut because it is the square of *c* and is similarly related to *d*, but it is worth ruling out if you have nothing better to go on. Incidentally, you have already seen these answers in an earlier question. My dredging up this answer sequence for a second time underlines the fact that many questions can be approached simultaneously by more than one Rule, and that on any given question some Rules will be more applicable than others.

But do you remember which Rule easily solves this problem and what the preferred guess was?

If you said Look for the Nuclear Answer (Rule 5, page 51) and *c*, you are right. It is also worth mentioning that your success or failure here in recalling the "correct" procedure is predictive of whether you will be able to put the material in this book to good use on a real test. It's easy to spout back applications of a Rule while it is being discussed, but on a real test, you will perhaps find yourself severely unnerved by the relentless barrage of questions and by time pressure. You won't be able to say, "Hmm, that must be Rule 5, or maybe it's a Center of Symmetry. Now, was I supposed to avoid the center or choose the center?? And maybe I should look for a disguised non-answer while I'm at it." Etc., etc. Not at all. You'll be making these perceptions in split seconds, effortlessly—it is hoped—and in most cases without even talking to yourself about it. So the better you *know* the Rules, the more useful they will be in the heat of battle. Accordingly, if your performance in this unanticipated "review quiz" did not satisfy you, you may find it worthwhile to backtrack to the earlier Rules at this point and/or to read the ensuing material a bit more deliberately.

2. In the accompanying figure, if Q, R, and S are points on segment PT, the distance from the midpoint of QS to the midpoint of PT is

P	Q	R	S	T
⊢—77—→	39	64	75	

Note: Figure not drawn to scale.

(a) 0
(b) 1
(c) 2
(d) 3
(e) 128

It's hard to believe, but this question, with a classic monster, is from a real SAT test. The monster is, of course, *e*. You can drop it from consideration, and you are left with a Rule 3 situation (Center of Symmetry) on the remaining choices. (Did you realize that for yourself?) Thus, the best guess is that the answer is either *b* or *c*. If you then go so far as to apply Rule 1 (Avoid Ace), you'll be left with an answer of *b*. (Did you also make that connection?) The answer *is* actually *b*. More than 80 percent of the test takers missed it.

RULE 7

STANDARD
MULTIPLE-CHOICE
QUESTION

PUT IT TO A VOTE!

Let the distribution of answer choices themselves "elect" the correct answer.

MEMORY AID:

Vote

There is a rather peculiar question type that appears in both the Math and Verbal SAT's and in many other tests as well, although sometimes in a slightly altered format. Its structure is as follows:

Q: Which of the following statements is/are true?
I. Statement X
II. Statement Y
III. Statement Z

(a) I only
(b) II only
(c) III only
(d) I and III only
(e) II and III only

(The range of particular answer choices varies widely and may include other combinations of the statements such as "I and II only," "I, II, and III," and "None.")

This question type, which I will call the "True/False Battery," comes up only a handful of times in an entire SAT but is worth special mention because it is particularly vulnerable to an indirect-solving method.

The method calls for simply conducting a little "election"—with the help of the answer choices provided by the test maker. You will be able to "cast your vote" for the one *they* elect. For example, polling the answer choices given in the sample question above, you would find a total of:

Two votes for Statement I (in choices *a* and *d*)

Two votes for Statement II (in choices *b* and *e*)

Three votes for Statement III (in choices *c*, *d*, and *e*)

The winner of the election, therefore, is statement III, and thus any answer containing statement III is preferable to one that does not contain statement III. Accordingly, reviewing the five answer choices with this in mind, we find that the best choices would be *c*, *d*, and *e*.

When an election is won *outright* by a single statement, as in the present case, the odds strongly favor that the answer choice containing the winning statement *alone* is the correct answer. Thus, in terms of the present example, the best choice would be *c*.

However, when there is a tie in the voting between two of the statements (such as an outcome of 3-3-2), all answer choices containing either or both of these statements are good guesses, and the answer choice containing *both* of them is *slightly* preferable to any of the others. For example, consider this answer configuration:

(a) I only
(b) II only
(c) III only
(d) I and II only
(e) I, II, and III

The outcome of this election would be:

Three votes for Statement I

(in *a, d,* and *e*)

Three votes for Statement II (in *b, d,* and *e*)

Two votes for Statement III (in *c* and *e*)

In this case, the answer choices containing statements I and/or II, specifically choices *a, b,* and *d,* are the most probable (rule out choice *e* because it contains a "loser" as well), and of these three answer choice *d* is slightly to be preferred because it splits its vote between the two winning statements.

WHY THIS RULE WORKS

Rule 7 (Vote) is actually a reincarnation of Rule 5 (Nuclear Answer) applied to the special case of True/False Batteries. It works as a Rule because the test maker is again concentrating his smoke screen around a single correct answer, and so we may again expect to find the correct answer where the smoke is densest. In the effort to maximize his chances of fooling you in this format, the test maker selects wrong answer choices that *overlap* or *partially contain* the correct answer. Thus, if he is trying to conceal a correct answer of "II only," he will be less inclined to surround it with unrelated answers like "I only," "III only," "I and III only," and "None" than with confusing answers like "I and II only," "II and III

only," and "I, II, and III." So once again, in his zeal to conceal the answer, he reveals it—at least to those who know how to look for it. And in this case, "looking for it" simply means holding an election.

HOW AND WHEN TO USE THIS RULE

Apply this Rule to all questions of the True/False Battery type which you are unable to answer directly. The format is unmistakable and, in the SAT at least, invariably consists of three statements (numbered I, II, and III) followed by the five answer choices (lettered, as usual, *a, b, c, d,* and *e*). In other tests, the format may vary slightly to accommodate a different number of statements and/or answer choices, but the task is essentially unchanged.

The process of conducting the election requires no discretion; you need only count. Every time one of the three statements is mentioned in an answer choice, whether alone or in company with another statement, you simply count one vote for that statement. Then add up the votes for each statement, determine the winning statement or statements, and select the answer or answers that best reflect the election results. If it's a toss-up among more than one answer choice, you will have to venture a guess, but as often as not, a single winner will stand out.

EXAMPLES

1. If quadrilateral ABCD has sides of lengths x, x, y, and z (not necessarily in that order) and angles of degree measures 90, 90, p, and q (not necessarily in that order), which of the following must be true?

    I. ABCD is either a rectangle or a square
    II. $p + q = 180$
    III. $y = z$

(a) II only
(b) I and II only
(c) I and III only
(d) II and III only
(e) I, II, and III

You conduct an election. The results are:
    Statement I: 3 votes (in *b*, *c*, and *e*)
    Statement II: 4 votes (in *a*, *b*, *d*, and *e*)
    Statement III: 3 votes (in *c*, *d*, and *e*)
The "winning" statement is II. The best guess, containing II alone, is *a*. (The actual correct answer is *a*.)

2. If $\dfrac{P}{M} = \dfrac{H + k}{T + k}$,

where P, M, H, T, and k are positive real numbers, which of the following is (are) true?

    I. If T>H, then M>P

    II. If T = 2H, then M = 2P
    III. If T = H, then M = P

(a) I only
(b) II only
(c) III only
(d) I and III only
(e) I, II, and III

The results of the election are:
    Statement I: 3 votes (in *a*, *d*, and *e*)
    Statement II: 2 votes (in *b* and *e*)
    Statement III: 3 votes (in *c*, *d*, and *e*)
The winning statements are I and III. The best guesses, containing statements I and/or III, are *a*, *c*, and *d* (*e* is disregarded in this case since it contains a "loser," Statement I), but especially *d* since it alone contains *both* winning statements. (The actual correct answer is *d*.)

In practice, the fact that an answer choice contains both winning statements makes it the favorite but not so strong a favorite as to recommend itself without qualification. It does, however, confer enough of an edge to be taken seriously (as we have done here) but one that must also be evaluated against other considerations such as Rule 1 (Avoid Aces).

Theoretically, there are a few situations in which an election will not produce a decisive result. For example:

(a) None
(b) I only

(c) II only
(d) III only
(e) I, II, and III

Election results: 2 for I, 2 for II, and 2 for III. But, I have never seen any of these come up on a real test, presumably because the test maker cannot resist making a good smoke screen.

PRACTICE QUESTIONS

1. xxxxxxxxxxxxxxxxxxxxx?
   I. xxxxxxxxxx
   II. xxxxxxxxxx
   III. xxxxxxxxxx

(a) None
(b) I only
(c) I and II only
(d) I and III only
(e) I, II, and III

The unusually lopsided vote of 4-2-2 makes answer choice *b* a very strong favorite.

2. xxxxxxxxxxxxxxxxxxxx?
   I. xxxxxxxxxx
   II. xxxxxxxxxx
   III. xxxxxxxxxx

(a) I only
(b) II only
(c) III only
(d) I and II only
(e) II and III only

The less lopsided but still decisive vote of 2-3-2 makes answer choice *b* the best guess.

3. xxxxxxxxxxxxxxxxxxxx?
   I. xxxxxxxxxx

II. xxxxxxxxxx
III. xxxxxxxxxx

(a) None
(b) I only
(c) II only
(d) III only
(e) II and III only

The tied vote of 1-2-2 means that statements II and III are equally probable, and therefore the most likely answer choices are *c* (II only), *d* (III only), and *e* (II and III only)—with an extra edge for *e* since it contains both winning statements.

Now that you've conducted a few elections for yourself, you may find it interesting and useful to note that Rule 2 (Avoid the Non-Answer) is completely consistent with Rule 7, since the non-answers "None" and "I, II, and III" (the equivalent of "All of the Above"—a superanswer) have no stake in and no effect on an election, and thereby automatically eliminate themselves from consideration.

This fact again underscores the interrelatedness of my system as a whole. The Rules are not isolated tips but correspond to actual facets of the test maker's mentality, and as such they work best when viewed as a synthesis and used in concert.

4. Previous two answers: *d*

If an asterisk (*) between two expressions indicates that the expression on the right exceeds the expression on the left by 1, which of the following is (are) true for all real numbers x?

   I. $x(x+2) * (x+1)^2$

   II. $x^2 * (x+1)^2$

   III. $\dfrac{x}{y} * \dfrac{x+1}{y+1}$

(a) None
(b) I only
(c) II only
(d) III only
(e) I and III only

Following two answers: *e*

The vote of 2-1-2 makes statements I and III equally probable winners, and thus the best guesses are *b* (I only), *d* (III only), and *e* (I and III only). Had it not been for the presence of *e* in the following two answers, answer choice *e*, which contains both winning statements, would have been a favorite. And had it not been for the presence of *d* in the preceding two answers, answer choice *d* would have been no worse than *b*. But the answer that makes the most sense is *b*. And it is correct.

5. Previous answer: *d*

According to the passage,* which of the following are statements of Plato's beliefs?

   I. Drama should expose the weaknesses of villains.

   II. Only those parts of Homer dealing with the heroes and gods may be used.

   III. Stories told to children should be strongly censored.

(a) I only
(b) II only
(c) III only
(d) II and III only
(e) I, II, and III

Following answer: *d*

The vote of 2-3-3 makes statements II and III equally probable, and therefore the most likely answer choices are *b*, *c*, and *d*. (Although it could be said that *e* likewise contains II and III, it has the defect of also containing I, a loser, so it should be ruled out.) The best of the three best choices would ordinarily be *d* because it contains both of the winning statements. But the presence of *d* in both neighboring answers makes *b* or *c* more likely (Rule I: Avoid Pairs). And since *ace* is also to be avoided when all else is equal (Rule 1), the best choice boils down to *b*. (The correct answer actually was *b*, though it's a bit academic in this case because we were skating on thin ice to arrive at it. Still, it's the best guess, even if it had turned out not to be the correct answer.)

███████

---

*This question, based on a long reading passage which needn't be reprinted here, is from the Verbal SAT and is included here among the Rules for math questions because the True/False Battery question type to which Rule 7 applies crops up not only on the Math SAT but in many and various testing situations.

RULE

8

STANDARD
MULTIPLE-CHOICE
QUESTION

ESTIMATE THE ANSWER

When you are at a loss for a more reliable technique in geometry and calculation problems—and especially when a diagram is given—make a visual estimate and test it against the answers given.

MEMORY AID:

Estimate

WHY THIS RULE WORKS

In his desire to complicate the essentially simple material he has to work with, the test maker often becomes so enamored of a particular finesse he has created that he overlooks the fact that the question is easily solved by completely sidestepping its subtlety. Of course, he is quite careful to arrange things so that you cannot arrive at an exact solution unless you understand his finesse, but thanks to the range of answer choices he provides, an estimated solution is often sufficient.

HOW AND WHEN TO USE THIS RULE

Certainly any time a diagram is given, the opportunity arises to use your eyes and your innate navigational sense in conjunction with logic and calculation. Often enough a question is *designed* to require visual assessment, but more often the test maker will use a diagram simply to illustrate something he needs to make clear in his question—while trusting that he will not be giving too much away and that you will not have enough sense—or nerve—to "eyeball it." (The figure that appears with example 1 under

Rule 5 is a good example of such a situation. You may now wish to return to it and solve it by Rule 8.) Of course, his grudging respect for your visual faculty does compel him to occasionally insert the caption, "Note: Figure not drawn to scale" when he feels an illustration could mislead you. But when the drawing could lead you—as almost any drawing can—he must remain silent or risk giving himself away even more. So any time you do *not* see the warning "Figure not drawn to scale," you should attempt to use the drawing to garner unintended clues, estimate a solution, and select the answer choice that is closest to your estimate. (When you *do* see the warning "Not drawn to scale," you can usually figure that the answer choice closest to a visual approximation will be *wrong*.)

As for *how* to estimate, it is an acquired skill which, like problem-solving itself, is neither always easy nor generally any harder than making the kind of educated guesses you make all the time in your life. ("Will this wad of paper hit the wastebasket at this angle?" or "Will I get through the amber light before it turns red?") Since each test question presents a different kind of problem as well as a different kind of opportunity, I will explain some typical techniques by means of ten varied examples from real tests. I could never explain all the techniques; they are as diverse as the question types themselves. The truth is that you will have to use your wits, but estimation is often an easier route to the answer.

EXAMPLES AND PRACTICE QUESTIONS

Try in each case to reach a direct solution to the problem first. This will give you an idea of how much work and time are at stake here. Then try to reach an estimated solution.

1. The accompanying figure shows a piece of paper in the shape of a parallelogram with measurements as indicated. If the paper is tacked at its center to a flat surface and then rotated about its center, the points covered by the paper will be a circular region of diameter

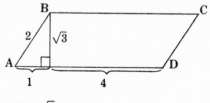

(a) $\sqrt{3}$
(b) 2
(c) 5
(d) $\sqrt{28}$
(e) $\sqrt{39}$

Your reading of the question tells you that you need to

determine the diameter of a circle equal to line AC in the diagram. You can *see* from the length of line AD that line AC must be a good deal longer than 5 and in all probability somewhat longer than 6. You then reinterpret the answer choices:

(a) less than 2
(b) 2
(c) 5
(d) a bit more than 5
(e) a bit more than 6

Is there any doubt, then, that *e* is the correct answer?

Admittedly, you had to get partway into the question to even set up the estimation procedure—but how often we find ourselves stumped, *partway* to a solution!

2. In the triangles in the accompanying figure, if AB, CD, and EF are line segments, what is the sum of the measures of the six marked angles?

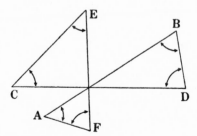

(a) 180°
(b) 360°
(c) 540°
(d) 720°
(e) It cannot be determined from the information given

You are looking at six angles located within three "fairly" regular triangles. (None of the triangles distinguishes itself by being exceptionally flat or elongated.) You should know that the sum of the three angles in any triangle equals 180°. One such angle would on average equal 60°, and six would on average equal 360°. Surely in the given illustration, with no perfectly regular triangles, the sum of six such angles could conceivably run as low as 240° or as high as 480°, but the only answers worth considering are *b* (360°) and *e* (It cannot be determined). Rule 2 (Avoid Non-Answers) argues against *e*, and though *e* should not be casually ruled out so long as you are unable to determine an exact answer, the best bet is clearly choice *b*. (The correct answer is *b*.)

3. In the accompanying figure, x =

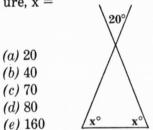

(a) 20
(b) 40
(c) 70
(d) 80
(e) 160

This is an easy question for many people to solve directly, but let's imagine you've been unable to do so, and must seek indirect means. None of the angles in the triangle appears to be more than a right angle

(90°). Therefore, since all three angles must total 180°, the only possible correct answers are *c* and *d*. That's not as good as a *real* solution (*d* is correct), but it's 150 percent better than not having a clue.

And don't forget your other resources. You may also have noticed that the answer progression 20-40-80-160 argues against choice *c* (70) according to Rule 5 (Nuclear Answer), and that the numerical closeness (*i.e.*, "smoke") of *c* to *d* points in favor of *d*.

4. In the accompanying figure, PQ and RS are diameters of circle O. If x = 30, then the ratio

$$\frac{\text{length of arc STQ}}{\text{circumference of circle O}} =$$

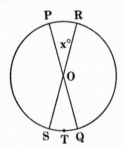

(a) $\frac{1}{12}$

(b) $\frac{1}{10}$

(c) $\frac{1}{9}$

(d) $\frac{1}{6}$

(e) $\frac{1}{3}$

Despite all the technical jargon, this one pretty much boils down to "What fraction of the pie is sliver SOQ?" If you try to cut up the rest of the pie (with your mind's eye or your pencil) into pieces of the same size as SOQ, you quickly see that *d* and *e* are out of the question, in that they represent a 6-piece pie and a 3-piece pie respectively. Furthermore, answer choice *c*, which would represent a 9-piece pie, is also out of the question because the full-diameter cuts already made force the pie to have an even number of (equal) pieces. Thus, the answer must be *a* or *b*. Your 50 percent chance of a right answer beats the average test takers, of whom only 45 percent got a right answer.

But once again, you can go further. In the present instance several other Rules can be called upon to help you decide between *a* and *b*. Rule 1 (Avoid Aces) favors *b*. Rule 3 (Center of Symmetry) also favors *b*. But the higher-numbered Rules 5 and 6, which together tell you to avoid the odd man out, come to a different verdict. Since answer choice *b* is the *exception* to the orderly progression 3-6-9-12 (in the denominators of the answer choices), answer *a* is indicated by the same logic that was brought to bear in the previous example. Remembering that when Rules conflict, it is best to go with the higher-numbered Rule, you choose *a*.* (The correct answer is *a*.)

---

*In practice you will find that it is not really necessary to remember the number of each Rule, but simply to have a rough idea of where they fall in relation to one another.

5. In the accompanying figure, if ABCD and EFGH are rectangles, what is the sum of the measures of the marked angles?

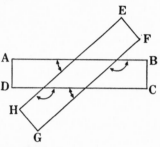

(a) 180°
(b) 270°
(c) 360°
(d) 540°
(e) It cannot be determined from the information given

Here you are asked for the sum of two acute (less than 90°) and two obtuse (more than 90°) angles. The law of averages would put the total somewhere around $4 \times 90°$ or 360°. Answer *c* is therefore the best bet. (The correct answer is *c*.)

6. If P is a point on line L in the accompanying figure and $x - y = 0$, then $y =$

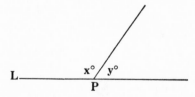

Note: Figure not drawn to scale.

(a) 0
(b) 45
(c) 90
(d) 135
(e) 180

Since an angle of 0° is no angle at all and an angle of 180° is a straight line, even the warning "not drawn to scale" cannot prevent us from eliminating *a* and *e*. However, the very presence of the warning does tell us that though angle y may *look* most nearly like 45°, we should be leery of this answer. Hence guess *c* or *d*. Consulting other Rules, we find that Rule 3 (Stay Close to the Center of Symmetry) and Rule 1 (Avoid Aces) are inconclusive, and it remains a toss-up between *c* and *d*. (The correct answer is *c*.)

7. How many 1-centimeter squares are required to make a border around the edge of the shaded square with a side of 8 centimeters as shown in the accompanying figure?

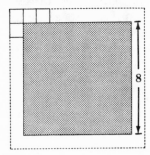

(a) 32
(b) 36
(c) 40
(d) 48
(e) 64

You can *see* that the shaded square will require 8 small squares on each of its four sides, for a total of 32, and that four corner squares will then be needed, for a grand total of 36.

The correct answer is *b*. The test maker probably intended the test taker to laboriously figure out that it was necessary to subtract 8^2 from 10^2, or else to blunder into the notion that he need only multiply 4×8 or 4×10. In this case, however, the indirect, "groping" solution is actually a lot easier than solving by equations.

8. Directions: This question consists of two quantities, one in column A and one in column B. You are to compare the two quantities and select your answer as follows:

(a) If the quantity in column A is greater
(b) If the quantity in column B is greater
(c) If the two quantities are equal
(d) If the relationship cannot be determined from the information given
(e) Does not appear at all as a choice in this kind of question

The question:

Lines L and M intersect as shown in the accompanying figure.

Column A	Column B
x	y

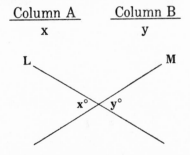

They *look* like they must be equal. The correct answer is *c*.

(This and the following question are of the type known as quantitative comparisons; these will be discussed in more detail under Rule 12.)

9. Directions: (Same as in previous question.)

Column A	Column B
Numbers of minutes in one week	Number of seconds in 7 hours

Although the unraveling of this problem is done not by means of geometry but by arithmetic alone (that is, it is not visual but purely mental), mental visualization can still be helpful. You could work this problem longhand, but mental manipulation of the data is really what's called for and will lead to a great time saving. There is no need to waste time by multiplying. Just state the number of units in each situation, and the problem solves itself at a glance:

60 minutes in an hour	60 seconds in a minute
24 hours in a day	60 minutes in an hour
7 days in a week	7 hours stipulated

The answer, after canceling a 60 and a 7 in each case, is clearly *b*. Remember, the test maker does not allow you much time per question. This should tell you that complex longhand calculations are not the keys to correct answers but can only be—whether intended or unintended by him—a trap for the lame.

10. In the accompanying figure, the area of square I is 25. The area of square II is 100. What is the area of square III?

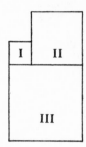

(a) 125
(b) 225
(c) 600
(d) 625
(e) 2500

Since square III is clearly larger than squares I and II combined, the answer cannot be *a* (125). Since square III is nowhere near six times as large as square II, the answer cannot be *c* (600), not to mention the even larger choices of *d* and *e*. Therefore answer *b* is a sure thing.

RULE

9

STANDARD
MULTIPLE-CHOICE
QUESTION

REVERSE GEAR

When in doubt about selecting from two or more answer choices, try each answer out experimentally if possible, to see if it meets the terms of the question. In other words, work backward.

MEMORY AID:

Backsolve

WHY THIS RULE WORKS

One of the answers must be right. The challenge and the opportunity are to find out which one it is by means of the elimination of the ones that it is not. In effect, you are taking hold of and yanking the partially raveled threads on the surface of the garment.

HOW AND WHEN TO USE THIS RULE

In algebra problems, the question often takes the form: "If such and such is true, then x = ?" If you ever find yourself unable to solve this kind of problem algebraically, or are the least bit uncertain about your solution, simply test each of the contending answer choices by "plugging" it into the equation presented in the question.

When you find one answer choice that resolves the equation, it will definitely be the right answer.

Although this Rule is most useful on algebra problems, it is applicable any time you find yourself unable to wrap your mind around an abstraction and need to make things more concrete.

EXAMPLES

1. If $x^3 = (2x)^2$ and $x \neq 0$, then x =

(a) 1
(b) 2
(c) 4
(d) 6
(e) 8

If your algebra isn't rusty, you'll have no trouble solving *directly* for the correct answer, which is c (4). But if, like 42 percent of the test takers on this real question who failed to come up with the right answer, you were uncertain about how to proceed, you could backsolve this quite easily as follows:

Testing each answer choice *in order* so as not to lose track of where you are, you would try *a* first and substitute its number (1) for x in the equation. Thus:

$$1^3 = (2 \times 1)^2$$
$$1 \times 1 \times 1 = 2 \times 2$$
$$1 = 4$$

Since 1 cannot in fact equal 4, you have proved that answer *a* is wrong. Proceed now to *b*, and substitute its number (2) for x in the equation:

$$2^3 = (2 \times 2)^2$$
$$2 \times 2 \times 2 = 4 \times 4$$
$$8 = 16$$

Again, since 8 does not equal 16, answer *b* is also wrong. Proceed to answer *c*:

$$4^3 = (2 \times 4)^2$$
$$4 \times 4 \times 4 = 8 \times 8$$
$$64 = 64$$

Eureka! Since 64 does indeed equal 64, that is, the equation is correctly balanced, the answer must be c.

It is interesting to note that this question also has Rule 3 (Center of Symmetry) characteristics, on the basis of which you may already have guessed that answers b, c, and d were the most plausible. If you had found yourself under time pressure in such a situation, you may have wished to save time by applying Rule 9's backsolving technique first to the answers that you already suspected were right.

2. If $\frac{7}{3}x = \frac{3}{7}y$ and $y \neq 0$,

   then $\frac{x}{y} =$

   (a) $\frac{9}{49}$

   (b) $\frac{3}{7}$

   (c) 1

   (d) $\frac{7}{3}$

   (e) $\frac{49}{9}$

You have already seen this question on page 56 in the discussion of Rule 5 (Nuclear Answer). If you do not remember or cannot reconstruct what we concluded about it, you have just failed my "surprise quiz." The conclusion drawn earlier was that the answer must be a, b, d, or e and that that was all the help we could get from Rule 5. So here is a perfect opportu-nity to press on with the help of Rule 9. Beginning with answer choice a, we find:

If $\frac{x}{y} = \frac{9}{49}$,

then x = 9 and y = 49.

Applying these values to the equation, we get:

$$\frac{7}{3} \times 9 = \frac{3}{7} \times 49$$

$$\frac{63}{3} = \frac{147}{7}$$

$$21 = 21$$

And we need go no further. The correct answer is a. More than three-quarters of the test takers missed this question!

3. If $x = \sqrt{y}$ and $y^2 = 64$, then x =

   (a) $\sqrt{2}$
   (b) $2\sqrt{2}$
   (c) 4
   (d) 8
   (e) 16

This question is more difficult, especially for people whose knowledge of square roots is weak. But even so, you can still backsolve this question. Begin by trying answer a on for size:

If $\sqrt{2} = \sqrt{y}$, then y= 2, and $y^2 = 4$.

But the question says $y^2 = 64$. Therefore x cannot equal $\sqrt{2}$, and choice a is ruled out. Try answer b:

If $2\sqrt{2} = \sqrt{y}$, then 4x2 = y, and $y^2 = 64$, as required.
Therefore, answer b is correct.

PRACTICE QUESTIONS

1. If a set of numbers is "quotiable," then the quotient $\frac{x}{y}$ of any two numbers x and y in the set is also in the set. One reason that the set (1, 3, 9, 27, 81) is not "quotiable" is that $\frac{27}{k}$ is not in the set. What is the value of k?

(a) 1
(b) 3
(c) 9
(d) 27
(e) 81

This question sounds frightening, but even if (like me) you aren't familiar with the lingo, you can still see that all you have to do is find a value of k which, when divided into 27, does not produce a member of the mentioned set. So, by trial and error:

1 into 27 is 27. Therefore, not *a*.
3 into 27 is 9. Therefore, not *b*.
9 into 27 is 3. Therefore, not *c*.
27 into 27 is 1. Therefore, not *d*.

And, whether arrived at by elimination or calculation, the correct answer must be *e*.

2. The accompanying figure shows a rod with black beads and white beads. How many beads must be slid from the right side to the left so that one-fourth of the beads on each side are black?

LEFT   RIGHT

○○●   ○●○○○○○○●○○

(a) 2
(b) 4
(c) 5
(d) 6
(e) 9

Yes, you've seen this one before, too (page 58). And you probably remembered that Rule 5 (Nuclear Answer) pointed strongly in the direction of *b* and *d*. But now by trial and error, you reason:

Slide two to the left (choice *a*) and two-fourths are black. Therefore, not *a*.

Slide four to the left (choice *b*) and two-sixths are black. Therefore, not *b*.

Slide five to the left (choice *c*) and two-sevenths are black. Therefore, not *c*.

Slide six to the left (choice *d*) and two-eighths (one-fourth) are black on the left side and one-fourth are black on the right side. Therefore the correct answer is *d*.

3. If $x + 4x^2 = 105$, then x =

(a) 2
(b) 3
(c) 4
(d) 5
(e) 6

Backsolve:

(a): $2 + 16 = 18$ not 105. Therefore, not *a*.

(b): $3 + 36 = 39$ not 105. Therefore, not *b*.

(c): $4 + 64 = 68$ not 105. Therefore, not *c*.

(d): $5 + 100 = 105$. Eureka!

RULE 10

STANDARD
MULTIPLE-CHOICE
QUESTION

PLUG IN NUMBERS AT RANDOM

Attempt trial solutions by assigning an arbitrary value to each unknown term.

MEMORY AID:

Plug In

WHY THIS RULE WORKS

The test maker assumes that only those test takers who have mastered the abstractions of algebraic notation will stand a chance when a problem deals with such abstractions. The test maker overlooks the fact that every abstract statement is simply a universal formulation of a set of particular, *concrete* cases. In fact, any abstraction he invents can be made concrete by your assigning an arbitrary value to it and observing its behavior in the "special case" that has thereby been created. Although the behavior of one special case is not *theoretically* conclusive, nevertheless—practically speaking—in a test situation it almost invariably points to the correct answer. When time permits, you can test a second and a third case, or exhaust the remaining answer choices by applying the same conditions to them in the style of Rule 9 (Backsolve).

HOW AND WHEN TO USE THIS RULE

If you find yourself lacking a means of direct solution in algebra problems, and generally whenever it is not convenient or possible to plug in the five answer choices as indicated by Rule 9, the most useful indirect procedure is to plug in numbers at random and see if a definite pattern emerges.

Although *any* numbers *could* be used for this purpose, the best set of numbers consists of *primes that cannot be combined to produce any other numbers in the set.* The simplest such set to use is 2, 3, 7, 11, 17, 41...But since you'll rarely have occasion to use more than three or four of them, you needn't bother to memorize beyond 2, 3, 7, 11.

I stress these particular numbers because they will produce the most unambiguous results. (As you will see, the order in which they are applied sometimes needs to be carefully thought out to avoid needless complications.) If you use numbers like 1, 2, 3, 4, 5, and 6, you may be left with some uncertainty about *how* you arrived at a particular result. For example, a result of 12 using the latter series might have been arrived at by adding $1 + 5 + 6$ *or* $2 + 4 + 6$, etc., *or* by multiplying 2×6 *or* 3×4; but in the former series the only route by which a result of 12 could have been arrived at is $2 + 3 + 7$. The reason for avoiding such ambiguities will become apparent as you put this Rule into use: Since you will be trying to isolate the unknowns, it makes sense to keep the "knowns" separate as well.

EXAMPLES

1. If a is not 0 or 1, what is the reciprocal of $\dfrac{a}{1 - \frac{1}{a}}$?

(a) $\dfrac{a - 1}{a^2}$

(b) $\dfrac{a - 1}{a}$

(c) $a - 1$

(d) $\dfrac{1}{a - 1}$

(e) $\dfrac{a^2}{a - 1}$

This question was bewilderingly abstract for most test takers. Fewer than 20 percent got the correct answer. We have already seen this question under Rule 5 (Nuclear Answer), page 51. Do you remember what was concluded at that time? But that was just a guess. Rule 10, on the other hand, can produce a *reliable* correct answer as follows:

There is only one unknown, "a," so we replace it with the first number of our special series, "2." When a = 2, the expression in the question becomes

$$\frac{2}{1 - \frac{1}{2}} = \frac{2}{\frac{1}{2}} = 4.$$

Now, since we are looking for the reciprocal of this expression, we need to find the answer choice which produces a value of 1 over 4 or $\frac{1}{4}$ when a = 2. And

we proceed to test each answer choice in the same way.

Answer choice *a* yields instant results:

$$\frac{2 - 1}{4} = \frac{1}{4},$$

precisely the answer we were looking for. Choice *a* is therefore *very probably* the correct answer. If we can show that none of the other answer choices produces this result, then *a* is definitely the correct answer. (If another answer produced the same result, which is a possible but highly unlikely outcome, we would then have to retest both contending answer choices with a different random value, say a = 3, and after one or two such extra tests, only one correct answer would remain for all cases. I mention this in order to be comprehensive, but I have *never* encountered a situation like this in real life, and it is not worth worrying about.)

If time is a factor, you may be content to have found the answer you were looking for (in the present case answer *a* with a value of $\frac{1}{4}$). But if time permits—and only if time permits—it will not hurt to exhaust the four other answer choices, or to test the probable correct answer by a second random-number substitution, just to assure yourself that you haven't stumbled into a special case or an arithmetical error. So, plugging in a = 2 for the remaining answer choices, you get:

(b) $\frac{2-1}{2} = \frac{1}{2}$.

Therefore, not b.

(c) $2 - 1 = 1$.

Therefore, not c.

(d) $\frac{1}{2-1} = 1$.

Therefore, not d.

(e) $\frac{4}{2-1} = 4$.

Therefore, not e.

Therefore the answer is definitely a.

The fact that the expressions in both c and d produced an identical result (1) when a = 2 underlines the possibility already mentioned that random numbers can play tricks on you. But fortunately there was no duplication of $\frac{1}{4}$, the target answer!

At this point it is not really necessary to conduct additional random-number substitutions, but if we had wanted to test our answer a different way, we could have let a = 3, a = 7, and so on, in both expressions to be tested (the one in the question and the one in answer a). Thus, if a = 3:

Q: $\dfrac{3}{1-\frac{1}{3}} = \dfrac{3}{\frac{2}{3}} = \dfrac{9}{2}$

A: $\dfrac{3-1}{3^2} = \dfrac{2}{9}$,

the reciprocal of $\dfrac{9}{2}$.

If a = 7:

Q: $\dfrac{7}{1-\frac{1}{7}} = \dfrac{7}{\frac{6}{7}} = \dfrac{49}{6}$

A: $\dfrac{7-1}{7^2} = \dfrac{6}{49}$,

the reciprocal of $\dfrac{49}{6}$.

2. If p, q, and r are integers and $\frac{q}{p}$ and $\frac{r}{q}$ are both integers greater than 1, which of the following is *not* an integer?

(a) $\dfrac{p}{r}$

(b) $\dfrac{r}{p}$

(c) $\dfrac{rp}{q}$

(d) $\dfrac{rq}{p}$

(e) $\dfrac{qr}{rp}$

In order for $\frac{q}{p}$ and $\frac{r}{q}$ to be integers greater than 1, as the question stipulates, we must select our random numbers rather carefully. So:

Let p = 2.
Let q = 2 × 3 (that is, 6) so $\frac{q}{p}$ produces the integer 3.
Let r = 2 × 3 × 7 (that is, 42) so $\frac{r}{q}$ produces the integer 7.

It is important to note that we could not simply have let q = 3 and r = 7, the next two numbers in our sequence, because the terms of the question would thereby have been violated.

This fact points up the need for choosing "random" numbers quite carefully. Now, testing these assigned values against the answer choices, we find that:

(a) $\frac{2}{42}$ is *not* an integer, and therefore the correct answer. Just for the practice of it, test the remaining answers for yourself. All should produce integers and reconfirm *a* as the correct answer.

3. If the average of v and w is p and the average of x, y, and z is q, what is the average of v, w, x, y, and z in terms of p and q?

(a) $p + q$

(b) $\dfrac{p + q}{2}$

(c) $2p + 3q$

(d) $\dfrac{2p + 3q}{5}$

(e) $\dfrac{3p + 2q}{5}$

You have seen this question before. Do you recall what Rule applied and what you were able to guess at that time? (See page 57, if you have forgotten.) But now you can go one step further —to certainty. Applying Rule 10, you can replace the seven variables in the question with your "favorite" random numbers:

Let v = 3
Let w = 7
Let x = 2

Let y = 11
Let z = 17

Therefore $p = \dfrac{v + w}{2^*} =$

$\dfrac{3 + 7}{2} = 5.$

And $q = \dfrac{x + y + z}{3^*} =$

$\dfrac{2 + 11 + 17}{3} = 10.$

Notice that I have altered the usual *order* of the random numbers from 2-3-7-11-17 to 3-7-2-11-17 in order to arrive at clean whole numbers for the variables p and q. Selecting the random numbers with a view toward how they combine with one another can save a great deal of computation time. But apart from that, the *order* is in any case unimportant.

We can now see that the "target value" for the average of v, w, x, y, and z, which we will be trying to locate in one of the answer choices, is

$\dfrac{3 + 7 + 2 + 11 + 17}{5^*}$ or 8.

And, testing the answer choices against the target value of 8, we find:

(a) $5 + 10 = 15.$
Therefore, not *a*.

(b) $\dfrac{5 + 10}{2} = 7\frac{1}{2}$
Therefore, not *b*.

---

*The starred number is the number of items averaged in each case above.

(c) $10 + 30 = 40$.

Therefore, not *c*.

(d) $\dfrac{10 + 30}{5} = 8$.

Therefore, the correct answer is *d*.

(e) (purely as a formality)

$\dfrac{15 + 20}{5} = 7$.

Therefore, not *e*.

4. The sum of ten numbers is what percent of the average of the ten numbers?

(a) 0.001%
(b) 2%
(c) 10%
(d) 200%
(e) 1,000%

Sometimes, as in the present case, the problem requires you to develop a general rule. The easiest way to do this is to plug in random numbers in *successive* operations and observe the pattern that develops. Here, since we are *not* asked for ten *different* numbers, we can make do with any *one* of our random numbers in each successive operation. So, we try two or three:

The sum of ten 2's = 20, and the average of ten 2's = 2.

The sum of ten 3's = 30, and the average of ten 3's = 3.

The sum of ten 7's = 70, and the average of ten 7's = 7.

From this we can develop a general rule that the sum of any ten numbers will always be ten times the average of the same ten numbers. And since that average number, like any number, is 100 percent of itself, ten times it is 1,000 percent of it. Therefore the answer is *e*.

5.   AB
      + AB
      ‾‾‾‾
        CD

A, B, C, and D are different digits in the correctly worked sum of 2 two-digit numbers above. If A and B are even numbers and if B is equal to twice A, then C is

(a) 2
(b) 4
(c) 6
(d) 7
(e) 9

It is not always possible to plug in our favorite random numbers. Here the very specific terms of the problem require us to abandon 2, 3, 7, 11, but we can still test-solve with plugged-in numbers. (Indeed, that is the *only* way, to my knowledge, that this problem can be solved.)

Since A and B are *even* numbers and B is twice A, the only possible values for A and B are either 2 and 4, respectively, or 4 and 8, respectively. We can test-solve for each hypothesis:

If A = 2 and B = 4, then AB + AB = 48, in which case C = 4. But the problem states that C must be different from B, so this is an incorrect hypothesis.

Therefore A = 4 and B = 8, in which case C = 9 (48 + 48 = 96). The correct answer is thus *e*.

PRACTICE QUESTIONS

1. If $x + 2$ is an even integer, which of the following is NOT an even integer?

(a) $2x + 2$
(b) $2x + 4$
(c) $x - 2$
(d) x
(e) $x + 1$

If we let $x = 2$, the requirement in the problem that $x + 2$ be an even integer is met, since $x + 2$ would in that case equal 4. Testing the answer choices, we find:

(a) $4 + 2 = 6$, an even integer. Therefore a is incorrect.

(b) $4 + 4 = 8$, an even integer. Therefore b is incorrect.

(c) $2 - 2 = 0$, an even integer. Therefore c is incorrect.

(d) 2, an even integer. Therefore d is incorrect.

At this point, without even testing answer choice e, we know by elimination that it must be the correct answer. Still it is wise to test e just to be certain that we haven't made a mistake somewhere along the way:

(e) $2 + 1 = 3$, *not* an even integer, and therefore the correct answer.

Admittedly, many test takers would have *seen* the correct solution to this problem at a glance, and would find the procedure just outlined comi-cally extravagant in such a simple and obvious situation. In fact, nearly three-quarters of all test takers got this question right, presumably without going through any such rigmarole. But things are rarely this straightforward, as the next example shows. It was, not surprisingly, missed by more than 80 percent of all test takers. With the help of Rule 10, however, it boils down to a simplistic arithmetic problem, involving nothing more complex than the number 14. Can you solve it?

2. If $J = \dfrac{rK}{M + r}$, then $r =$

(a) $\dfrac{JM}{K - J}$

(b) $\dfrac{JM}{J - K}$

(c) $\dfrac{JM}{K - 1}$

(d) $\dfrac{M}{-K}$

(e) $\dfrac{M}{K}$

If we let $J = 2$, $K = 3$, and $M = 7$, we can easily solve for r in the original expression as follows:

$$2 = \frac{3r}{7 + r}$$

$$3r = 14 + 2r$$

$$3r - 2r = 14$$

$$r = 14$$

Applying these values to the answer choices, we get:

(a) $\dfrac{2 \times 7}{3 - 2} = 14,$

the anticipated value of **r**. Therefore a is the probable correct answer.

Just to be sure, we exhaust the other choices:

(b) $\dfrac{14}{-1} = -14.$

Therefore, b is incorrect.

(c) $\dfrac{14}{2} = 7.$

Therefore, c is incorrect.

(d) $\dfrac{7}{-3}.$

Therefore, d is incorrect.

(e) $\dfrac{7}{3}.$

Therefore, e is incorrect.

3. If $\dfrac{P}{M} = \dfrac{H + k}{T + k},$

where P, M, H, T, and k are positive real numbers, which of the following is (are) true?
I. If $T > H$, then $M > P$
II. If $T = 2H$, then $M = 2P$
III. If $T = H$, then $M = P$

(a) I only
(b) II only
(c) III only
(d) I and III only
(e) I, II, and III

We have seen this problem before. Under what Rule? What did we "conclude" at that time? (If you've forgotten, check page 68.) But, whatever the guessing odds, we can now plug in our favorite random numbers to test each of the three "If/then" statements with certainty.

I. If $T = 3$, $H = 2$, and $k = 7$, then $M = 10$ and $P = 9$. Therefore, since T is greater than H and M is greater than P, statement I is *true*.

II. If $T = 4$ (that is, 2H), $H = 2$, and $k = 3$, then $M = 7$ and $P = 5$. Therefore, $T = 2H$ but M does not equal 2P, and statement II is *false*.

III. If $T = 2$, $H = 2$, and $k = 3$, then $M = 5$ and $P = 5$. Therefore, $M = P$, and statement III is *true*.

And since I and III only are true, the correct answer is d.

■

RULE 11

STANDARD
MULTIPLE-CHOICE
QUESTION

GET THE PICTURE

Represent the *known* quantities by drawing a diagram, and the unknown quantity will often reveal itself in your diagram.

WHY THIS RULE WORKS

The previous Rule works because the test maker discounts your ability to get the handle on an abstraction by means of *numbers*. The present Rule works because he underestimates your ability to get the handle on it by means of a *graphic* device.

HOW AND WHEN TO USE THIS RULE

Like Rules 9 and 10, this Rule is not a guessing technique but a fully reliable indirect solving method. It is most useful when you are able to understand the question but can't see your way clear to an algebraic formulation of it. The actual techniques for applying the Rule depend on the question itself and are best illustrated by example.

EXAMPLES

1. The meter in a taxicab registers $0.50 for the first $\frac{1}{5}$ of a mile and $0.10 for each additional $\frac{1}{5}$ of a mile. How many miles is a trip for which the meter registers $2.50?

(a) 5

(b) $4\frac{4}{5}$

(c) $4\frac{3}{5}$

(d) $4\frac{2}{5}$

(e) $4\frac{1}{5}$

If you found yourself hard put to solve this real problem algebraically, it may come as a relief to know that you could solve it just as well and probably just as quickly by drawing a schematic. To do this, you simply translate the wording of the problem into picture form. In the present case, you would draw a line (as shown) to represent the taxicab's progress, and draw lines across it to represent the accumulated distance and meter reading. You would label the first line $\frac{1}{5}$ mile and $0.50; the second $\frac{2}{5}$ mile and $0.60; the third $\frac{3}{5}$ mile and $0.70; the fourth $\frac{4}{5}$ mile and $0.80; and the fifth 1 mile and $0.90. You could then continue marking every $\frac{1}{5}$ mile this way until you reached a meter reading of $2.50; or, in the present case, you could save time by marking only each additional full mile and adding $0.50 to the meter (since the meter is ticking at a constant rate) until you approached the target number of $2.50, at which point you could resume marking fifths of a mile until you reached $2.50 exactly. As the diagram clearly shows, the correct answer is $4\frac{1}{5}$ miles, or answer choice e.

2. In the currency of the country of Ug, 15 dops are equal to 1 tif. If 10 dops equal 1 decadop, what is the value in tifs of 6 decadops?

(a) $\frac{1}{15}$

(b) $\frac{2}{5}$

(c) $\frac{3}{2}$

(d) 3

(e) 4

In many cases, such as in this real example, the schematic method can get you over the rough spots in the reasoning process and lead you to a routine arithmetical solution. Your diagram might take the form of comparative value scales and look like this:

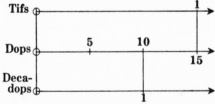

Now that is not a *complete* solution, and you could theoretically extend the scales until you arrived at one, but at this point we are already able to see quite clearly that 1 decadop = $\frac{10}{15}$ or $\frac{2}{3}$ tif and that if we were to extend the scale to 6 decadops they would equal $6 \times \frac{2}{3}$ tifs. Either way, this potentially baffling algebra problem, properly handled, becomes routine. The answer is 4 tifs, answer choice *e*.

PRACTICE QUESTIONS

1. When purchased, a bottle with a 10-ounce capacity contains 8 ounces of soda. If the buyer drinks 6 ounces of the soda, then what percent of the bottle is empty?

(a) 20%
(b) 25%
(c) 60%
(d) 75%
(e) 80%

We have seen this problem before (on page 54 under Nuclear Answer) and concluded at that time, with some reservation, that the best *guess* was answer choice *e*. Now you can proceed to solve it and eliminate all doubt. Your schematic might look like this:

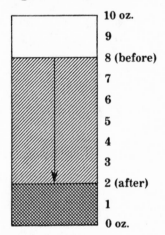

Of course, now it is easy to see that, with $\frac{2}{10}$ or 20% of the bottle full, 80% is empty. But would you believe that more than half of all test takers got this problem wrong?

2. After John gave 6 marbles to Bill, they each had the same number of marbles. John originally had how many more marbles than Bill?

(a) 3

(b) 6

(c) 9

(d) 12

(e) 15

Selecting a number at random, which in this case needs to be larger than 6 to satisfy the terms of the question (say, 7 or 11 as recommended in Rule 10), we diagram the problem as follows:

AFTER

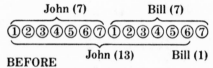

DIFFERENCE: 12

Therefore *d* is the correct answer.

RULE 12

QUANTITATIVE COMPARISONS

TAME A WILD GUESS ON QC's

• Avoid CDE columns, especially D (No-Man's Land) and E (a blunder).
• Avoid identical answers on successive questions.

MEMORY AID:

Avoid CDE, Pairs, and Triplets

Quantitative comparisons are the second of the two types of problems that occur in the Math SAT. We have already had previews of this question type under Rules 2 and 8. QC's consist of two quantities, one in column A and one in column B. You are asked to compare the two and decide:

(a) if the quantity in column A is greater;

(b) if the quantity in column B is greater;

(c) if the two quantities are equal;

(d) if the relationship cannot be determined.

Thus, instead of the usual five answer choices, there are only four. The answer sheet continues to have a *place* for marking all five letters *(a, b, c, d,* and *e)*, but you are expected to *remember* that the last answer choice is *d* and not *e*. There is no question that some people make the mistake of continuing to mark *e* in the belief that they are marking *d*. *Be especially careful about this.*

Since there are only four answer choices it is generally more difficult to eliminate choices here than in the standard five-part multiple-choice format; nevertheless, many questions break down to a clear choice between answers *a* and *b*, or between answers *c* and *d*.

Of the eleven Rules presented thus far, only Rules 8, 10, and 11 (Estimate, Plug in, Diagram It) will continue to be useful in QC's. Rules 3 through 7 and Rule 9 simply do not apply to this question format. (Don't feel as though you have to memorize any of this information; in practice, when a Rule applies or can be applied, it will *present itself* in the moment of truth, purely by mental association, if you have understood this book well.) Rules 1 and 2 are in essence still valid for QC's, but they will be entirely reformulated here in terms of this particular question type. In addition, a few Special Tips for QC's will follow Rule 12.

FURTHER EXPLANATION

The "Avoid Aces" principle (Rule 1, part 1) must of course be revised for four-part questions, while at the same time the terrain of "No-Man's Land" (as defined in Rule 2) turns out to have widened markedly. Both answer choice *c* ("The two quantities are equal," *i.e.*, neither is greater) and especially answer choice *d* ("The relationship cannot be determined") exhibit non-answer qualities to some extent and should therefore be avoided in your attempt to tame a *wild guess* only. (And it goes without saying that answer choice *e* is literally out of the question.) So *cde* becomes the trio to avoid on

QC's, rather than *ace* as formulated in Rule 1 for standard multiple-choice questions. Apart from that, procedures for applying Rule 12 are exactly as outlined under Rules 1 and 2, pages 26 and 34. Examples of QC's appear in the Special Tips below. Remember also, as stated in Rules 1 and 2, that if you have *good reason* to pick answer *c* or *d*, do not hesitate to do so; they do, after all, account for 45 percent of all correct answers in the tests I have analyzed.

SPECIAL TIPS FOR QC's

Remember, you are asked to compare:
(a) if the quantity in column A is greater;
(b) if the quantity in column B is greater;
(c) if the two quantities are equal;
(d) if the relationship cannot be determined.

1. Look for sneaky, even illogical questions:

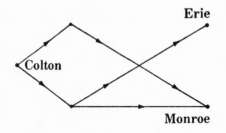

Column A	Column B
The total number of ways you can go from Colton to Erie if you follow the arrows on the map	The total number of ways you can go from Colton to Monroe if you follow the arrows on the map

If turns are allowed at the crossroads—a point not resolved by the wording of the question—then there are two ways to go from Colton to Erie and three ways from Colton to Monroe. But if not, then there is only one way from Colton to Erie and two from Colton to Monroe. In either case the answer would be *b*. But it is easy to confuse the two possible readings of the question in midcount, as I myself did, and come up with an incorrect answer of *c*. Or to imagine that the two roughly equal routes from Colton to Erie as against the single sensible route from Colton to Monroe (who would ever go out of their way?) indicate an answer of *a*. Or to conclude that, given all the ambiguity in the question, the relationship cannot be determined, and that answer choice *d* is therefore indicated. But *b*, according to the test maker, is the only correct answer.

By the way, this is a classic example of the point I make on page 15. Look for "Everyman's" answer, which will be neither overly abstruse nor profound.

2. Look for the tricky use of algebraic signs:

Column A	Column B
n	$(-1)n$

n is an integer

Unless we realize that integers can be both positive and nega-, tive and that we are *not* told that n is necessarily a positive integer, we may erroneously conclude that the answer is *a*. But, in fact, the answer is *d* because the sign of n can't be determined.

3. Look for incongruities to distinguish other candidates for choice *d*.

We have already seen an example of these in the QC example presented under Rule 2, page 40. Here is another:

Column A	Column B
Area of a triangle with altitude 4	Area of a triangle with base 5

You just know there's not enough information here, as the illustrations show.

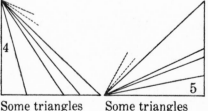

Some triangles with altitude 4   Some triangles with base 5

The necessity for including this awkward kind of question points to the test maker's embarrassment over having a functionally weak answer choice *d*.

4. Save time by avoiding calculations:

Column A

$23^2 + 2 (5)(23) + 5^2$

Column B

$23^2 - 2 (5)(23) + 5^2$

The calculations in the above problem are, typically, not so difficult that you couldn't work them out in a minute or so, but a careful look at the terms reveals that the only difference between columns A and B lies in the operation sign preceding the second term. Since a positive quantity is always more than a negative quantity, the correct answer is clearly *a—at a glance.* Time saved: enough to answer one extra question.

RULE 13

ANTONYMS

DEFINE AND SUBSTI- TUTE

Isolate the essential meaning of the main word by giving as precise a definition or synonym of it as you can. If the correct answer is still not apparent, do the same for each of the answer choices.

WHY THIS RULE WORKS

This Rule is the first to apply exclusively to the Verbal SAT and has been devised for antonym questions such as:

GOOD:
(a) Sour
(b) Bad
(c) Red
(d) Hot
(e) Ugly

The test maker does not construct antonym questions out of thin air but makes them up according to a "recipe" or formula. He does this because he has no choice in the matter. Antonym questions are by definition nothing more than little equations. Although they are found in the verbal section of the SAT, they are as much math problems as they are word problems. This section and Rule are aimed primarily at math-strong, word-weak students who find it helpful to quantify verbal meanings. Word-strong, math-weak students needn't pay as much attention to the material that follows, and if they find it confusing should ignore it or be amused by it accordingly. Antonym problems follow the basic equation: $x = -(-x)$. That is, "antonym" means "equals the negative of," $(= -)$, and an equivalent of the first word (x) will be found among the answer choices *with sign reversed* $(-x)$. This means that you can solve an antonym as you would a math problem, by simply substituting terms in either side of the equation. (In the simplistic example shown above, you would of course not need to "solve" anything to realize that the opposite of "good" is "bad." But real antonym questions are rarely this simple or clear-cut. And although the test maker rarely, if ever, uses a word you have never seen before, he tends to choose words that vocabulary-weak students have heard, are unsure of, and have *always meant to look up.* A question on a real-life test might look more like this: GOOD: *(a)* Sour *(b)* Heinous *(c)* Red *(d)* Hot *(e)* Ugly, with choice *b* still the best answer even though it is only *approximately* an antonym of "good.") In effect, Rule 13 is nothing more than a restatement of Rules 9 and 10 for use with verbal problems: *Plug in* equivalents and then *Backsolve* if necessary.

HOW AND WHEN TO USE THIS RULE

Sometimes the equation $x = -(-x)$ will already be apparent in the question, as in the following two examples (which 96 percent of all test takers answered correctly):

STALE:
(a) Noticeable
(b) Fresh
(c) Dainty
(d) Moist
(e) Genuine

(Answer b "fresh" is obviously
−x in relation to "stale.")

CONCEAL:
(a) Examine
(b) Recognize
(c) Expose
(d) Pronounce
(e) Arise

(Answer c "expose" is obviously
−x in relation to "conceal.")

But more often the correct answer will not be so screamingly obvious. Take the following question for example:

VENTURESOME:
(a) Lacking agility
(b) Lethal
(c) Fragile
(d) Timid
(e) Without significance

Let's imagine that you find answer choices a, c, and d all equally plausible because all could in some sense be seen as opposed to "venturesome." Since a clear winner has not presented itself, you apply Rule 13 and try to think of synonyms for venturesome. Three come easily to mind: "bold," "daring," and "adventurous." When you again consult the answer choices armed with these synonyms, you find no new support for a or c but strong confirmation of d ("timid") thanks to these equivalents of x.

Use this Rule on all antonym questions that pose a problem for you; it has the virtue of not consuming a great deal of time, and there is no better indirect way to solve this kind of question.

EXAMPLES

1. EQUILIBRIUM:

(a) Opposition
(b) Insignificance
(c) Lack of freedom
(d) Lack of contact
(e) Lack of balance

The most obvious synonyms of "equilibrium" are "balance," "poise," and "composure." Perhaps not all of them would have occurred to you in the heat of battle, but any one of them would have pointed strongly to e. It is interesting to note that the presence of the words "lack of" in three of the answer choices and the negative prefix "in-" in a fourth answer choice catch the test maker red-handed in his use of formulas. Such words and prefixes are simply representations of the second minus sign in $x = -(-x)$. Many antonym questions contain answer choices that have more than one word in them and they will frequently, though not always, be useful to you in this way.

2. DOUBTFUL:
(a) Practical
(b) Consistent
(c) Nonexistent
(d) Impervious
(e) Unquestionable

(Note the three negative prefixes.) The synonyms of "doubtful," in various senses, are "uncertain," "unbelieving," and "questionable." And answer *e* immediately stands out as a good antonym for at least two of them. Notice that adding or subtracting negative prefixes to either the main word or any of the answer choices can be a very effective way of applying Rule 13. The negative of "doubtful" is "indubitable," a good synonym of "unquestionable"; the negative of "unquestionable" is "questionable," a good synonym for "doubtful."

3. STIFF:
(a) Limber
(b) Melted
(c) Succulent
(d) Twisted
(e) Silky

Here, as is frequently the case, the simple mathematical aspect of antonyms is compounded by a possible obscurity in the words used. For, unlike numbers, not all words are easily "readable." In the present case, for instance, it is quite conceivable that some test takers will not know the precise meaning of "succulent." If you ever find yourself not knowing all the words, forget about the one(s) you don't know and be content to play the substitution game with the ones you do know. If you come to a satisfactory solution, you may disregard the unknown word. It is often planted there just to disconcert you anyway, and perhaps waste your time or bully you into a wrong guess. But if you can come to no satisfactory answer choice among the known words, then *do* guess that the correct answer is the unknown word (or guess randomly from among the unknown words if there are more than one). Thus, in the present case, it does not matter if you do not know the meaning of "succulent." Knowing that "stiff" is "firm," "rigid," "tense," you need go no further than answer choice *a* ("limber"), which is very nearly an exact antonym of two of these three. You may pause over "melted" ("soft") and "silky" ("smooth") and even "twisted" (opposite of "straight"), but none of the antonyms of these words ("hard," "rough," and "straight," respectively) fits "stiff" precisely. And with "succulent" an unknown, "limber" remains as the best gamble—and hardly a gamble at all.

4. PARTISAN:
(a) Commoner
(b) Neutral
(c) Unifier
(d) Ascetic
(e) Pacifist

Here the meaning of the *main* word ("partisan") may escape some test takers. This is of course the most difficult situation of all. Imagine that you do not know exactly what "partisan" means. You have a vague notion that it means something like "partial to one side," or "some kind of a guerrilla" but that still leaves the issue in doubt. On the basis of your hunch, the answer could well be *b* ("neutral"), *c* ("unifier"), or *e* ("pacifist"), not to mention *d* ("ascetic") whose meaning is perhaps also unknown to you. In such a situation it is best to guess only from among those choices which seem plausible on the basis of your knowledge and ignore all the others. In other words, guess from among *b*, *c*, and *e*. (The correct answer is *b*.)

The odds of there being both an obscure main word and an obscure correct answer on any given question are very slim. Such a situation is carefully avoided by the test maker, because his vital interest in maintaining a wide spread of scores prevents him from wanting too many wrong answers— except perhaps on the last two or three items in a section. (You will recall that on the SAT the items in each section are arranged generally by increasing order of difficulty—therefore, only on the last two or three items in a particular section does the probability increase that both words will be at least a bit obscure.)

On those occasions when you do find yourself totally at a loss, remember that you still have Rule 1 (page 26) to fall back on. Also, the situation in example 4 somewhat resembles the situation covered in Rule 5 (Nuclear Answer, page 51). For purposes of guessing, the presence of two or three kindred and equally plausible words tells you that one of those words is probably the correct answer. (You may have observed a similar echo of Rule 5 in example 1 on page 100, wherein three answer choices beginning with the words "lack of" are a clue that one of them is probably the correct answer.)

PRACTICE QUESTIONS

1. COAT:
(a) Take off
(b) Strike hard
(c) Open wide
(d) Watch closely
(e) Work diligently

Although "coat" may have several meanings, the fact that all five answer choices are verbal forms suggests that the desired meaning is "to cover," "to overlay," "to put on." Therefore the best answer is *a*. Although "coat" also could mean "protect" here, suggesting a possible relationship to answer *b*, the opposition of the two ideas is not very strong or precise. Likewise a meaning of "enclose" or "cover over" is not a convincing enough opposition to choice c.

2. DISCREPANCY:
(a) Decision
(b) Attribute
(c) Restriction
(d) Clarification
(e) Concordance

Clearly this question is as much a test of vocabulary as of logic, but assuming you were not at a loss for the meaning of the words, you could have reasoned as follows: "Discrepancy" can mean "variance" or "disagreement." Only choice e provides a synonym whose antonym fits that meaning: "harmony" or "agreement." Thus it was necessary to substitute synonyms for both the main word and an answer choice before their relationship came into clear focus: $x = -(-x)$. Discrepancy (= disagreement) = −concordance (= agreement). Disagreement = −agreement.

3. FERMENTING:
(a) Improvising
(b) Stagnating
(c) Wavering
(d) Plunging deeply
(e) Dissolving

Since "fermenting" means "in a state of being activated or agitated (as by yeast or bacteria)," only choice b, which refers to a state of motionless-ness, provides a suitable antonym.

4. DEPRESS:
(a) Force
(b) Allow
(c) Clarify
(d) Elate
(e) Loosen

Among the many meanings of "depress," only the meaning of "sadden" or "discourage" suggests a properly contrasting relationship with any of the answer choices, in this case d ("elate").

In addition to this Rule, Rule 1 (Avoid Aces), page 26 also applies to antonyms and Rule 5 (Nuclear Answer), page 51 is occasionally helpful.

RULE 14

ANALOGIES

DEFINE AND DIAGRAM

Define the essential relationship between the main pair of terms as precisely as possible, *or* illustrate it in a diagram. Then test your definition or diagram against each pair of answer candidates.

WHY THIS RULE WORKS

As with the previous question type, antonyms, the test maker must create his analogy questions according to a definite "recipe," because in essence they too are a simple mathematical equation. The basic equation as in the example that follows is

$$\frac{A}{B} = \frac{C}{D}.$$

YAWN:BOREDOM::*

(a) Dream:Sleep
(b) Anger:Madness
(c) Smile:Amusement
(d) Face:Expression
(e) Impatience:Rebellion

That is, the relationship that the first term bears to the second term (the main pair) will be the same as the relationship the third term bears to the fourth term (the correct answer pair). The two pairs of terms will be related in each case in a very specific and consistent way. Most errors on this question type are made because of flabby thinking at this pivotal point. The way in which the terms are related will, of course, vary from question to question, but the correct answer to any given question will

*Double colòn :: means "as"; therefore the example above can be read: Yawn (is to) Boredom "as" (a) dream (is to) sleep, etc.

depend on your being quite clear about the kind of relationship involved. A list of these relationships appears on the following page.

The upshot of all this is that you can "solve" an analogy question by determining the nature of the main relationship and then seeking out an identical relationship among the five pairs of answer choices. In effect, Rule 14 is nothing more than a restatement of Rule 11 (page 90) for use with verbal problems: Spell out or get a picture of the relationship.

Of course, analogy questions, like antonym questions, are not always purely mathematical but are often also a test of vocabulary and other information as well. (The Miller Analogies Test or MAT, discussed in a later section [page 129], is a tedious 100-question extravaganza consisting of nothing but this question type and is as much a test of knowledge as of logic.) Still, unless you have a firm grasp of the operational aspect of this question type, you will be at a disadvantage.

HOW AND WHEN TO USE THIS RULE

Always. There is no other systematic approach to analogy questions.

LIST OF COMMON TYPES OF ANALOGIES:

Equality (or synonymity)
  (TALL:HIGH)
Opposition (TALL:SHORT)
Description (MIDGET:SHORT)
The part and the whole
  (WOMAN:HUMANITY)
Cause and effect (RAIN:FLOOD)
Process (TADPOLE:FROG)
Companionship (HAM:EGGS)
Function (BROOM:SWEEP)
Use (SAW:CARPENTER)
Manufacture (CLOTH:COTTON)
Relative size (RIVER:CREEK)
Intensity (REQUEST:ENTREAT)
Sequence (MORNING:
  AFTERNOON)
Measure (INCH:DISTANCE)
Purpose (FOOD:NUTRITION)
Origin (CHICKEN:EGG)

EXAMPLES

1. RIVER:CREEK::

(a) Street:Alley
(b) Hill:Tunnel
(c) Path:Sidewalk
(d) Hedge:Fence
(e) Island:Peninsula

Define the relationship of the main pair: A river is like a creek, only bigger, so the relationship is one of relative size. Or, if you cannot define the relationship in words, try to diagram or symbolize it. Whether actually written on paper or viewed in the mind's eye, the diagram of the main pair might look like this: "R:c," in which the relative size of the initials for the two words river and creek symbolizes their fundamental relationship. (Of course, you may use whatever symbols or diagrams make sense to you. There is no "alphabet" of symbolism to learn.)

Now, having completed the analysis of the main pair, you can readily see that the only answer choice that fits the definition or the diagram we have made is choice *a* (Street: Alley), of which it could be said, "A street is like an alley, only bigger," or "S:a." No other answer choice conforms to the relationship that has been spelled out in either the definition or the diagram.

2. AMPLIFIER:HEAR::

(a) Turntable:Listen
(b) Typewriter:Spell
(c) Platter:Eat
(d) Camera:Feel
(e) Microscope:See

Define the relationship of the main pair: An amplifier makes it easier to hear by magnifying sound. Or diagram it: a→(sS)→h, which is to say, an <u>a</u>mplifier makes <u>s</u>ound into <u>S</u>OUND to improve or benefit <u>h</u>earing.

Now, if the correct answer has not already popped out for you, you may wish to test each answer choice against this formulation: Does a turntable make it easier to listen by increasing something? No. There is, of course, a similarity in subject matter with the main pair, but the resemblance ends there. Does a typewriter make it easier to spell by increasing something (say, speed or neatness)? Hardly. Does a platter make it easier to eat by increasing something? Well, a platter suggests large size, but not necessarily an improvement of anything. Does a camera make it easier to feel? Ridiculous. Does a microscope make it easier to see by increasing something (say, the apparent size of an object)? Yes, a more or less perfect fit $(m \rightarrow (oO) \rightarrow s)$. The answer is e.

3. HOMESTRETCH: RACE::

(a) Finale:Opera
(b) Goal:Contest
(c) Boundary:Journey
(d) Terminal:Station
(e) Platform:Campaign

Define the relationship: Homestretch is the final section or portion of a race. Or diagram it:

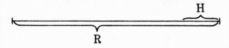

The correct answer, as will perhaps be immediately apparent now, is a (finale:opera), because the finale is the final section or portion of an opera.

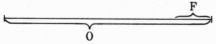

Note that b (goal:contest), which may otherwise seem a plausible answer, is shown to be faulty by the discrepancy in its diagram:

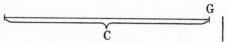

4. THIMBLE:FINGER::

(a) Muzzle:Snout
(b) Collar:Neck
(c) Bracelet:Wrist
(d) Helmet:Head
(e) Yoke:Shoulder

Define the relationship: A thimble encloses and protects a finger from injury. Or diagram it:

with the arrow symbolizing potential injury in this case. Checking the answers, we may now ask: Does a muzzle enclose and protect a snout from injury? Well, this almost makes it but not quite, because the muzzle actually prevents the snout from injur*ing* rather than protecting it from injury. Does a collar protect a neck? Hardly. Does a bracelet protect a wrist? Not usually. Does a helmet enclose and protect a head from injury? Yes, precisely.

And does a yoke protect a shoulder? No, it simply harnesses its power. Thus d is the correct answer.

This question points up the importance of stating the essential relationship as completely and precisely as possible. All five answer choices suggest the idea of enclosing. If our definition and symbol had simply said/shown "a thimble encloses a finger," we'd probably have gone astray.

PRACTICE QUESTIONS

1. CEDAR:WOOD::

(a) Textile:Silk
(b) Copper:Metal
(c) Porcelain:Dish
(d) Lace:Dress
(e) Clay:Brick

Your definition of the main relationship should have gone something like this: "cedar is a kind of wood," and your diagram might have looked like this:
wwwwwww...or this ⟨ C) W ⟩ .
|
C

When you tested the answer choices, you should have concluded that "a textile is not a kind of silk," but quite the opposite (this reversal of the relationship is a common test maker's trap!); that copper is indeed a kind of metal; that, although a dish can be made of porcelain, porcelain is not strictly a kind of dish; that lace and dress are similarly inexact; and that clay and brick fail for the same reason. And thus you should have had no trouble recognizing the answer, *b.*

MMMMMMM...or ⟨ C) M ⟩ .
|
C

2. FLURRY:BLIZZARD::

(a) Trickle:Deluge
(b) Rapids:Rock
(c) Lightning:Cloudburst
(d) Spray:Foam
(e) Mountain:Summit

Your definition of the relationship might have been "the least and the greatest extremes of snow." Your diagram: f:B!, or something to that effect. You should then not have had to seek beyond answer choice *a* for the correct answer, whose pair of terms represent the least and greatest extremes of rain (t:D!). In this light, all the other choices are inappropriate, and do not conform to either the definition or the diagram.

3. SPATULA:ICING::

(a) Trowel:Mortar
(b) Knife:Bread
(c) Sieve:Flour
(d) Spoon:Bowl
(e) Straw:Milk

Your definition: "A spatula is a tool for applying icing to a cake." Your diagram:

Your trial solution of the answer choices: "A trowel is a tool for applying mortar to a brick." (Looks good.) "A knife is not a tool for applying bread to anything." "A sieve is not a tool for applying flour so much as it is a tool for processing flour." "A spoon is not a tool for applying a bowl to anything." And "a straw is hardly a tool for applying milk to something, even if a contrived argument can be made for applying milk to the mouth by a straw." So the choice *a* is the only one that makes any real sense, and the only one that is at all consistent with the diagram:

4. BARREN: PRODUCTIVITY::

(a) Torrid:Warmth
(b) Innocuous:Harm
(c) Aberrant:Change
(d) Prodigal:Reform
(e) Random:Originality

Your definition: Apart from the fact that barren is an adjective and productivity is a noun, they are simple opposites. Your diagram: B (adj)<———>P (n). To simplify your search, you may read the second member of each answer choice as an adjective and simply look for opposites: Torrid and warm are not opposites. Innocuous (which means "harmless") and harmful are clearly opposites. Aberrant (which means unpredictable) and changeful are almost synonyms. Prodigal (which means wasteful) and reforming have no particular relationship at all. And random and original

are an equally dubious pairing. Granted that you needed some vocabulary skill to solve this particular question, still *nothing* was possible until you properly defined the slightly complex relationship between the main pair of terms.

In addition to this Rule, Rule 1 (Avoid Aces), page 26, continues to apply and Rule 13 (Define and Substitute), page 98 is occasionally helpful.

RULE 15

SENTENCE
COMPLETIONS

ANTICI-PATE THE ANSWER

As you read the sentence, look for clues in its structure or rhythm that tell you what kinds of word(s) will be best suited for filling in the blank(s). Guess at the answer even before consulting the choices. One will likely match or approximate your guess.

WHY THIS RULE WORKS

Most sentence completions are simply exercises in verbal architecture, tests of your dexterity with the nuts and bolts of sentence construction. That's pretty much all they *can* be, given their structure, and that's all the test maker tries to put into them. For example:

> Although its publicity has been _____, the film itself is intelligent, well-acted, handsomely produced, and altogether _____.
>
> *(a)* tasteless...respectable
> *(b)* extensive...moderate
> *(c)* sophisticated...amateur
> *(d)* risque...crude
> *(e)* perfect...spectacular

In each sentence he plants one or two clues, and a careful reading of them can lead to one and only one correct conclusion. The conclusion may be a function of logic, syntax, rhetoric, or semantics, but it is usually based on a purely mechanical trick.

HOW AND WHEN TO USE THIS RULE

Simply *look* and *listen* for the "birdie." It is remarkable how often the clue takes the form of a simple correlative conjunction or preposition like "because," "since," "for," "so," "and," "even if," "rather than," "which," "never...but always...," "although," "not...but...," etc. The three main themes to look for are cause, contrast, and coordination. An example of each will be given below. Together they account for 100 percent of sentence completions, in roughly equal proportions of frequency.

EXAMPLES

Cause (and effect): This type of birdie is distinguished by the following pattern: "Since X is so, then Y is so," or else "Y is so because X is so." It will often contain the words "since" or "because" in a causal clause and/or a word like "so" in a result clause.

> **1.** Engineers have long _____ that magnetic tape would _____ standard phonograph records, since it wears longer and is difficult to scratch.
>
> *(a)* predicted...replace
> *(b)* warned...destroy
> *(c)* admitted...ruin
> *(d)* lamented...surpass
> *(e)* charged...outsell

The presence of the word "since" tells you that the words you select for the blanks must make both parts of the sentence consistent in the sense of cause and effect. Furthermore, it is clear from both the structure of the sentence and a glance at the answer choices that the first blank must be filled by a verb of saying. Since the sentence speaks in terms of the relative merits of tapes and records rather than in terms of a physical confrontation between the two, we can rule out any notion of destruction or ruin (as expressed by choices *b* and *c*) and anticipate an idea of outperforming (as in choices *a*, *d*, and *e*). Alert readers will notice, in addition, that Rule 5 (Nuclear Answer on page 51) might be applicable here. Now, since there is no indication that the engineers are in any way emotionally involved, their lamentations and charges (choices *d* and *e*) would seem to be quite beside the point, and thus answer choice *a* stands out as a clear winner.

An important and useful corroborating point here is the *sound* of the completed sentence. With the blanks filled in by the words in answer choice *a*, the sentence is smoothly literate. All the other choices have an awkward ring to them.

Contrast (or negative cause): This type of birdie can be heard by the pattern, "Although X is so, nevertheless Y is also so," or "Not X but Y." It will often contain the words "although," "even if," "never...but always...," "rather than," etc.

2. The excitement does not _____ but _____ his senses, giving him a keener perception of a thousand details.

(a) slow...diverts
(b) blur...sharpens
(c) overrule...constricts
(d) heighten...aggravates
(e) forewarn...quickens

It is clear from the words "not...but..." that we are looking for two contrasting verbs, and it is clear from the descriptive clause that the second blank needs to be filled by a word indicating keenness of perception. Only answer choice *b* passes both of these tests. (Note the similarity of this to antonym questions!)

Coordination: This type of birdie comes in pairs of mutually supportive statements, often taking the form of apposition, a descriptive clause, a relative clause, and so on. The only word clues that are at all predictable are "and" and "which," but these do not occur with any great frequency.

3. Many predatory animals are remarkably _____, crouching motionlessly for hours until they detect potential prey.

(a) energetic
(b) vicious
(c) fleet
(d) patient
(e) massive

Clearly the blank must be filled in this case with a word described by the clause that follows it. Only answer choice *d* will do.

PRACTICE QUESTIONS

1. They argue that the author was determined to _____ his own conclusion, and so he _____ any information that did not support it.

(a) uphold...ignored
(b) revise...destroyed
(c) advance...devised
(d) disprove...distorted
(e) reverse...confiscated

The presence of the word "so" tells you that you are dealing with a causal relationship. This wonderful example can actually be broken down into a little math problem. Before even looking at the answer choice you can rephrase the sentence: "...the author was determined to *plus* his own conclusion, so he *minused* any information that did not support it." Evaluating the underlying meanings of the answer choices in terms of positive or negative algebraic signs, you can easily see the following:

(a) $(+)...(-)$ That is, "uphold" implies a positive value and "ignored" implies a negative value.
(b) $(-)...(-)$
(c) $(+)...(+)$
(d) $(-)...(-)$
(e) $(-)...(-)$

Thus the only answer choice that works algebraically is *a*, and it is, of course, correct.

Certainly I do not mean to advise you to literally work out such elaborate procedures in the heat of battle, but the entire process if performed mentally would only take a few seconds. Notice also the relative smoothness of the sound of the various answer choices when they are plugged into the sentence.

2. The questions raised by man's aspirations and wonderments, his creativeness, desires, and appetites, are _____, the answers relatively few.

(a) legion
(b) rhetorical
(c) academic
(d) inscrutable
(e) bizarre

The rhetorical contrast in the main statement, "Questions are _____, answers are few," obviously calls for a word like "many." Of course, part of the problem here is in identifying which of the five somewhat unusual answer choices means "many." Choice *a* ("legion") is correct. Choices *b*, *c*, and *d* are a good use of smoke on the test maker's part because they are not in everyone's vocabulary and all *seem* to go plausibly with the word "question." But it is the opposition to "few" that is being asked for here and not the stylistic compatibility with "question." Fewer than 20 percent of all test takers realized this.

3. Certain strong individuals believe that they have the right to _____ ordinary people, that they are _____ the moral responsibility that weighs upon the rest of us.

(a) inveigh against... held by
(b) trample over... exempt from
(c) lead about... restrained by
(d) argue with... confused by
(e) infiltrate among... critical of

The repetition of the words "that they" makes it clear that the second clause is an amplification or clarification of the first. Thus the meaning of the two clauses must be synonymous or at least compatible with each other. Before consulting the answer choices we may hypothesize from the context something like "overpower... free from," and we are not surprised that answer choice *b* neatly confirms this to be correct. None of the other answer choices make any sense at all in this context and all are simply a test maker's exercise in obfuscation.

In addition to Rule 15, other Rules that may help you on sentence completion questions are Rule 1 (Avoid Aces), page 26, Rule 5 (Nuclear Answer), page 51, and Rule 9 (Backsolve), page 78.

RC'S
READING COMPREHENSION QUESTIONS

This is the last of the four question types which appear on the Verbal SAT. It would take several pages and serve no purpose to present a complete example of this type of question here. Generally, a long reading passage consisting of several hundred words on a topic in the sciences or social studies is followed by a series of five or six questions based on the content of the passage. Two examples of the questions only are given at the end of this section.

1. As previously mentioned, this question type is generally regarded by test makers and test takers alike as the most difficult and time-consuming of all question types. Therefore, since all questions are of equal value, RC's should always be left for last so as not to put a strain on your CATS ratio (see page 17).

2. Always read the questions *before* attempting the reading passage, even though they appear last. This is especially helpful when a passage deals with a subject area with which you are not familiar.

Circle the crucial information requirements in the questions. Then read the passage and look back occasionally at the circled words. When you find corresponding ideas in the passage, circle them as well for easy reference, but read the passage through if time permits before answering any of the questions.

3. Be selective if necessary. There are bound to be some basic information questions (easy) and some inferential questions (hard) in every series of questions. An example of the former:

Q: The script employed in which of the following languages is characterized by letters of uniform thickness?

(a) Turkish
(b) Latin
(c) Egyptian
(d) Greek
(e) Swahili

And an example of the latter:

Q: The passage suggests that the influence of writing tools on letter forms

(a) is analogous to that of materials and technology on architecture

(b) is demonstrably greater than that of the prevailing culture and mores

(c) was unusually important to the development of hieroglyphics and their derivatives

(d) is considerable only in comparison to the impact of customs and economics

(e) became subordinate with the advent of the broad, sharp-edged pen

As you can see, there's quite a difference between the two types, and the easier ones can usually be spotted by their relative brevity. The correct answers to these questions (which happen to be d and a respectively), could only have been gleaned from the information in the reading passage I have not supplied.

My point is: Make sure you attempt the easy ones first, and write off or guess at the hard ones if necessary. Many people, including myself, score well over 700 without doing well on these few inferential questions, perhaps even because they don't waste time on them.

In addition to these tips, other Rules that may help you on the reading comprehension questions are Rule 1 (Avoid Aces), page 26, and on the true-false battery questions, which make an occasional appearance in this test section, Rule 7 (Vote), page 65.

RULE 16

SENTENCE
CORRECTIONS

LEAST IS BEST

When in doubt, select the shortest or next-to-shortest answer choice. Of the two, all other things being equal, give a slight preference to the next-to-shortest.

WHY THIS RULE WORKS

Rule 16 for Sentence Correction questions and the information on page 119 for Usage Questions are all that you will need to handle the Test of Standard Written English (TSWE), part 3 of the SAT. For some not-so-strange reason, fully 87 percent of the correct answers to sentence corrections are found in the shortest and next-to-shortest answer choices. As in the following example, answer choices are not arranged according to length, so it is impossible to predict which letter choices these will be, but you can simply examine the various answer choices and select either one of the shortest two.

If you think the underlined phrase is correct, select answer a; *otherwise select the answer that produces a more effective sentence.*

Q: Unless they take action soon, the world may face a power struggle for the resources of the sea.

(a) Unless they take action
(b) Unless action is taken
(c) Unless action will be taken
(d) If it will not take action
(e) If action will not be taken

By doing this, your guessing odds will increase by 117 percent! The simple reason that this Rule works so effectively is that English is a very terse language, and the best ways to express things are usually also the shortest ways. The test maker clearly has not reckoned with this fact at all.

You will of course not be able to anticipate the complete answer in most cases, but you will often know intuitively and immediately what the first word of the correct answer will have to be. In the example below, you can quickly find the correct answer, *d,* because in reading the question you already sense that you are looking for an answer beginning with the word "they."

Q: Books like "Gulliver's Travels" and "Robinson Crusoe" were written for adults, but also becoming children's classics.

(a) also becoming children's classics
(b) a children's classic is what they have become too
(c) since they have become children's classics
(d) they have become chil-dren's classics
(e) having become children's classics too

HOW AND WHEN TO USE THIS RULE

The application of this Rule couldn't be simpler. The two examples already given should suffice to illustrate how to use it. Refer to them and try to find the shortest and next-to-shortest choices. In the first example the shortest is *b* and the second shortest is *a*. (Recall that the correct answer was *b*, and that *a* is a bad *guess* in any case.) In the second example the shortest was *a* and the second shortest was *d*. (Correct answer was *d*.) The fact that these examples, which were initially selected without reference to Rule 16, handily illustrate the Rule is no coincidence; with 87 percent probability of following the Rule, they would be exceptional if they didn't.

It is worth noting that a context could be imagined in which more than one answer choice is correct in a given sentence. For example, it is not inconceivable, in the first example, that answer choice *a could* make sense, assuming a previous sentence in which it is made clear who "they" are. But it is important to select the most *internally* consistent answer choice.

In addition to this Rule, other Rules that may help you on sentence corrections are Rule 1 (Avoid Aces), page 26, and Rule 2 (Avoid the Non-Answer), page 34, again in effect because each question contains an answer choice of "no change" (answer choice *a* in questions of this type). An echo of Rule 16 is heard in Rule 4 (Go for Broke), page 46. Rule 9 (Backsolve), page 78, is fundamental to this question type in the same way as it was for sentence completions. Rule 15 (Anticipate the Answer), page 110, is also very much in effect.

◾◾◾◾◾

USAGE QUES- TIONS

These are basically a find-the-error exercise, a game similar to "What's Wrong with This Picture?" For example:

He spoke <u>bluntly</u> and <u>angrily</u>
             a   *b*
to <u>we</u> <u>spectators</u>. <u>No error.</u>
  c   *d*   *e*

The correct answer—because it is incorrect—is answer choice *c*.

Because this question type is full of bluffs and subtle traps:

1. Read carefully and critically with eye and ear. It may seem as if this should go without saying. But people actually miss questions like:

Q: <u>Although</u> the plan seemed
   a
<u>acceptably</u> to the officials in
   b
the Pentagon, the White

House <u>declared</u> it inadequate.
       c   *d*
<u>No error.</u>
 e

The correct answer—because it is incorrect—is *b*. Many test takers evidently read "acceptable" for "acceptably" because that is what their grammatical sense told them to see, and were misled into selecting answer choice *e* (No error).

2. Don't be put off by a slight awkwardness or inelegance. Such lapses are common. The correct answer to the following question is *e* (No error):

Q: A good many modern mu-

sicians <u>have begun</u> <u>compos-</u>
       a   *b*
ing pieces that <u>call for</u> using
           c
electronic devices <u>as</u> musical
             d
instruments. <u>No error.</u>
        e

3. Don't be put off by factual errors or opinionated statements. The usage questions are only meant to test usage. The correct answer to the following question is *d*.

Q: <u>Unless</u> bilingual and bicul-
  a
tural programs are developed

<u>and funded</u>, the school dis-
   b
trict will not be <u>able to meet</u>
             c
the needs <u>for</u> all of its stu-
       d
dents. <u>No error.</u>
     e

In addition to these tips, other Rules that may help you on usage questions are Rule 1 (Avoid Aces), page 26, and Rule 2 (Avoid the Non-Answer), page 34 because each contains as an answer choice *e*—No error.

PART 3

CBAT'S AND OTHER TESTS

CBAT'S

COLLEGE BOARD ACHIEVEMENT TESTS

The College Boards are given in fifteen subject areas and vary somewhat in format from subject to subject. The majority of questions in all the tests are five- or four-part multiple-choice questions. All the tests consist, at least in part, of reading comprehension question types, though the reading passages are generally not lengthy and usually call for knowledgeable interpretation of facts rather than simple comprehension of what is stated.

As mentioned in "The Testing Game" (page 9), achievement tests are generally less susceptible to indirect methods of attack than are aptitude tests, but since most students who take the College Boards take the SAT at the same time, the benefits gained by studying this book for the SAT will naturally carry over to the achievement tests. But whenever knowledge of factual material is the primary object of the game, indirect methods will of course have correspondingly less value— though it would be hard to imagine a test that is not in some significant way vulnerable to indirect attack.

Large portions of the achievement tests in math and the sciences closely resemble the Math SAT test, with much of the challenge coming in the areas of computation and analysis. Therefore, students preparing for such tests should study Rules 1 through 12. The English Composition Achievement Test is a carbon copy of TSWE and therefore calls for a study of the material in the TSWE section (page 116).

In addition, most of the achievement tests make ample use of the true/false battery question type—in one form or another—so Rule 7 (page 65) becomes particularly valuable.

So much for similarities. There are a few structural differences between achievement tests and the SAT. These will require two small amendments to previous Rules and a single new Rule for an entirely new question type, the mix and match.

AMENDMENT TO RULE 1

On the achievement tests you will be confronted with four-part multiple-choice questions. The only difference between five-part multiple-choice questions and four-part multiple-choice questions is the absence of a middle (symmetrically neutral) column. All the psychological qualities of the two end columns discussed under Rule 1 (Avoid Aces), page 26, remain in effect. Therefore, the translation of the "Avoid Aces" Rule into four-part multiple-choice situations is, when guessing wildly, simply to avoid choices *a* and *d*. The potency of this amended version of Rule 1 is somewhat less than the original, but it is still of significant value (a 5.6 percent to 28 percent edge in random samples) when you are reduced to wild guessing. Note: This does not apply to Quantitative Comparisons, which are a special case and are covered by Rule 12 (page 94).

Avoiding identical answers on successive questions still applies on the CBAT's.

AMENDMENT TO RULE 7

Many of the true/false battery questions in the achievement tests will be identical in format to the ones dealt with under Rule 7 (Put It to a Vote!), page 65, in that they will have *three* statements to evaluate and five combinations of them to choose from. In these cases, which are. numerous in some of the tests, you can apply Rule 7 with all the usual confidence.

There will be some questions, however, in which four or more statements will be given, and the five answer choices will become correspondingly more complex. For example:

Q: If _____, then which of the following are true?
I. xxxxxxxxxx
II. xxxxxxxxxx
III. xxxxxxxxxx
IV. xxxxxxxxxx
(a) I, II, and IV only
(b) III and IV only
(c) II and IV only
(d) IV only
(e) None of the above

Do not be put off by the increased complexity. You may still put the question to a vote, though the data may be a little more ambiguous and the Rule slightly less reliable than when only three statements are involved. The vote would be:
I. 1 vote *(a)*
II. 2 votes *(a* and *c)*
III. 1 vote *(b)*
IV. 4 votes *(a, b, c,* and *d)*
About all you can say in this case is that answer choice *d* (IV only) is a favorite, but *c* (II and IV only) cannot be entirely dismissed. With nothing else to go on, guess *d* and keep your fingers crossed.

■

RULE 17

MIX-AND-MATCHES

AVOID REPEATS ON MIX-AND-MATCHES

When guessing, avoid letters already used for other answers within the mix-and-match series. That is, return to a letter already used only when you are sure of your answer.

WHY THIS RULE WORKS

The mix-and-match battery question type, an example of which appears below, comes up in many achievement tests and is vulnerable to a special guessing technique.

> Directions: The group of questions below consists of five lettered headings followed by a list of numbered questions. For each numbered question select the one heading which answers the question correctly. Each heading may be used once, more than once, or not at all.
>
> (a) Alaska
> (b) Texas
> (c) Michigan
> (d) Rhode Island
> (e) Tennessee
>
> 1. Once belonged to Russia (Answer: a)
> 2. Once belonged to Mexico (Answer: b)
> 3. Smallest state (Answer: d)
> 4. Largest state (Answer: a)
> 5. Borders Great Lakes (Answer: c)
> 6. A river (Answer: e)

It simply would not make sense for the test maker to set up a series of five or six questions of the type shown above without making a fairly well-balanced use of the answer choices at his disposal. Since it rarely happens that any one answer choice is used more than twice in a given series, or that more than one answer choice is not used at all, your success in answering *some* of the questions in the series greatly increases your guessing odds on those that remain.

HOW TO USE THIS RULE

Having answered as many questions in the series as you could with any degree of certainty, simply guess the remaining answers from among the letters you have not previously used, or have used least.

EXAMPLES

1. In the sample question above, imagine that from your knowledge you had answered the first five questions with some assurance, and you were stuck on number 6. What letter should you guess? Having already used a twice, you can be pretty sure it will not occur a third time. And not having used e at all yet, you should put your money on e rather than b, c, or d. Admittedly, answer e is far from a sure thing, since the test maker has the option, and frequently uses it, of avoiding one or more letters entirely, but it is the best gamble under the circumstances.

Similarly, if you had answered all but number 2, your best bet on number 2 would be b; if you had answered all but number 3, your best bet on it would be *d;* and if you had answered all but number 5, your best bet would be *c.* But if you had answered all but number 1, *or* all but number 4, you would be able to derive no statistical advantage by answering *a* in either case even though *a* turned out to be the answer in both cases.

On the other hand, if you had answered all but numbers 1 *and* 4, a guess of *a* would be indicated in both cases, though you couldn't have dreamed that you would thereby be answering more than one correctly.

Now, I have of course loaded the deck by selecting some of the most favorable guessing situations (when only one or two questions in a series remain unanswered and there is good letter distribution among those already answered), and you will probably not be so consistently lucky in a real-life situation, but you will be increasing your odds by 20 percent or more, depending on the situation, whenever you use Rule 17.

2. In the sample question above, you have answered items 1 *and* 4. What should you guess on the others? You realize that *a* is now a very poor risk, so you guess wildly at anything but *a* for each of the remaining questions. Your odds increase by 20 percent.

3. In the sample question above, you have answered items 1, 2, and 3 successfully. What should you guess on the others? Rule out *a, b,* and *d* on each of the three remaining choices and guess *c* or *e,* and you will have increased your odds even more significantly than in the previous example.

OTHER TESTS

PSAT/NMSQT

The Preliminary Scholastic Aptitude Test (which also acts as the National Merit Scholarship Qualifying Test) was designed to prepare students for the SAT and is thus identical to the SAT in all respects, except that the TSWE is not included.

Students preparing for the PSAT/NMSQT should study Rules 1 through 15 and any miscellaneous Special Tips.

ACT

The American College Testing Program, a "rival" of the SAT, is requested as a supplement to the SAT score at some colleges, and supplants it entirely at others. The ACT consists of five-part multiple-choice math questions, four-part multiple-choice reading comprehension and factual questions in the natural and social sciences, and a form of sentence-correction question that is a cross between the sentence corrections and usage questions found on the TSWE.

Study Part I, plus Rules 1 through 11 (except for Rule 7), Rule 16 (page 116), the Usage Tips (page 119), and the Amendment to Rule 1 (page 123).

AP/CLEP

The Advanced Placement Program and the College Level Examination Program of the College Board have similar objectives (basically, exemption from or credit for college course work), and they make use of tests of similar format. Both are achievement-type tests that come in many varieties (a total of seventy-two different tests in a wide range of subject areas), which consist in most cases exclusively of five-part multiple-choice questions that test your knowledge of a specific subject area. They closely resemble College Board Achievement Tests and the SAT.

Study Part I and Rules 1 through 11 only.

GRE

Graduate Record Examinations consist of a general aptitude test and a range of achievement tests in specific subject areas. They are the big brothers, respectively, of the SAT and the College Board Achievement Tests, bearing the same relationship to graduate school admissions as the former do to college admissions.

Their various formats include five-part and four-part multiple-choice questions, reading comprehension passages, analogies, and true/false and mix-and-match batteries.

Study Parts I and II, except for Rules 12 and 13.

MAT

The Miller Analogies Test, a "rival" of the GRE, is requested as a supplement to the GRE score at some graduate schools, and supplants it entirely at others. It consists *only* of four-part multiple-choice analogy questions and is different from all the foregoing tests in that there is *no penalty* for incorrect answers. Your raw score (number of correct answers out of 100) is your final score. Therefore, it is extremely important to at least venture a guess—even a desperate guess—on every question. Failing to allow yourself a minute or so of "bail-out time" at the end of the test to fill in all remaining blanks in accordance with the Amendment to Rule 1 (page 123) could cost you dearly.

The analogy questions in the MAT differ in two significant ways from those that appear on the SAT:

1. Instead of being asked to complete the analogy by selecting the last *two* terms (see page 104) you are asked to select only *one* term, and its position in the formula varies from question to question. Thus there are four possible arrangements:

xxxx:yyyy::zzzz:_____
xxxx:yyyy::_____:zzzz
xxxx:_____::yyyy:zzzz
_____:xxxx::yyyy:zzzz

The blank in each case is to be filled in by selecting one of four answer choices provided and lettered *a, b, c, d*.

2. The subject matter is not restricted to vocabulary and semantics but varies widely among several disciplines, including general information, the humanities, the social and natural sciences, and even word-play.

Besides these tips, study Part I, plus Rule 1, second half, (page 26), Rule 14 (page 104), and the Amendment to Rule 1 (page 123).

SSAT

The Secondary School Aptitude Test comprises five-part multiple-choice questions in reading comprehension, sentence completions, and synonyms.

Study Part I, plus Rules 1 through 15 (except for Rule 12) and the Reading Comprehension (page 114).

GED

The Test of General Educational Development (High School Equivalency Exam) is an achievement test comprising five-part multiple-choice questions in mathematics, reading comprehension, usage and sentence corrections.

Study Part I, plus Rules 1 through 11, Reading Comprehension (page 114), Rule 16 (page 116), and Usage Tips (page 119).

THE REGENTS

The New York State Regents Examinations are achievement tests comprising four-part multiple-choice questions in a wide range of subject areas.

Study Part I, plus Rules 1 through 11, 15 and 16, and the Amendment to Rule 1 (page 123).

LSAT

The Law School Admission Test comprises five-part and four-part multiple-choice questions in reading comprehension and interpretation, sentence completions, sentence corrections, quantitative comparisons, and true/false batteries.

Study Part I, plus Rules 1 through 12, 15, Reading Comprehension (page 114), Rule 16 (page 116), the Amendment to Rule 1 (page 123), and Rule 17 (page 125).

MCAT

The Medical College Admissions Test comprises five-part, four-part, and even three-part multiple-choice questions, including SAT math-type ques-

tions in the natural sciences, true/false and mix-and-match batteries, and reading comprehension questions.

Study Part I, plus Rules 1 through 11, Reading Comprehension (page 114), the Amendments to Rule 1 (page 123) and Rule 7 (page 124), and Rule 17 (page 125).

DAT

The Dental Admissions Test comprises five-part and four-part multiple-choice questions and includes analogies, reading comprehension questions, and synonyms. Although we have not encountered synonyms on any of the tests mentioned up to this point, Rule 13 (page 98), which was designed for use with antonyms, will be useful if you think of synonyms as antonyms with the signs reversed.

Study Part I, plus Rules 1 through 14, Reading Comprehension (page 114), and the Amendment to Rule 1 (page 123).

GMAT

The Graduate Management Admission Test comprises five-part multiple-choice questions and is structurally very similar to the SAT without the TSWE and quantitative comparisons.

Study Part I, plus Rules 1 through 15 (except for Rule 12), and Reading Comprehension (page 114).

NTE

The National Teacher Exam comprises five-part and four-part multiple-choice questions and resembles a combined Math SAT, TSWE, and College Board Achievement Test.

Study Part I, plus Rules 1 through 11, Rule 16 (page 116), and the Amendment to Rule 1 (page 123).

PACE

The Professional and Administrative Career Exam comprises five-part multiple-choice questions, reading comprehension questions, and synonyms.

Study Part I, plus Rules 1, 2, and 13 (see the DAT, page 130, for use of Rule 13 with synonyms), and Reading Comprehension (page 114).

TOEFL

The Test of English as a Foreign Language comprises four-part multiple-choice questions in sentence completion, sentence correction, synonyms, and reading comprehension.

Study Part I, plus Rules 1, 2, 13, 15, 16, Reading Comprehension (page 114), and the Amendment to Rule 1 (page 123).

NURSING EXAMS

Both the National League for Nursing Exam and the Psychological Corporation Entrance Exam for Schools of Nursing consist of five-part multiple-choice questions, antonyms, synonyms, analogies, sentence completions, reading comprehension questions, and quantitative comparisons. Thus they are nearly identical to the SAT without the TSWE.

Study Part I, plus Rules 1 through 15 and Reading Comprehension (page 114).